Portuguese

Manuela Cook

TEACH YOURSELF BOOKS
Hodder and Stoughton

Contents

Contents

Introduction

This course of self-study aims to help you understand and speak simple Portuguese of the kind that you will need on a visit to a Portuguese-speaking country, and it has been designed particularly for your visit to Portugal, Madeira or the Azores. It cannot promise that you will be speaking perfect Portuguese after a few weeks, but by giving you the most important words and expressions you will need to use on your trip, it will enable you to get a great deal more out of your time abroad.

The course does not require a great deal of study or concentration, but it does offer more than a phrasebook and you will find that even if you can only manage an hour or two here and there in going through each unit, you will begin to acquire a basic knowledge of the language. Then take the book with you on your trip abroad, so that you can practise the words and phrases you have learnt. Don't be afraid to use them and enjoy the satisfaction of having been understood.

The course consists of 20 units, each dealing with a particular aspect of your visit. Each unit is based on carefully selected Portuguese words and phrases. Read them aloud, look at the English translations next to them, and refer back to the Pronunciation section where necessary. Then check your knowledge by doing the exercises. These are of two types. Some are merely a test of memory, to see whether you have remembered how to ask a question or repeat a phrase which occurred on a previous page. In others you are asked to adapt a given phrase or sentence in order to say what you want to say. If you find, gradually, that you are beginning to be able to do this, you are passing the 'acid test' of learning a language, which is being able to adapt given language patterns to any situation you choose.

At the end of each unit is a short information section in English which you will find useful on your visit.

The course expects very little knowledge of grammar, but readers who are interested in learning how the language works will find the introduction to Portuguese grammar useful. This contains some of the basic elements of grammar, mainly those illustrated in the course. A careful study of the Pronunciation section is advised, because although there can be no substitute for listening to Portuguese speaking their own language, it is possible to give a fairly good approximation of individual sounds. It is a good idea to read both these sections before starting the course, and then to refer to them frequently.

How to Speak Portuguese

1   Most Portuguese words are stressed on the last syllable but one:
    passa**por**te (*passport*)
2   Words which do not end in **a**, **e** and **o** are usually stressed on the last syllable:
    Portu**gal**
3   Words which are exceptions to the above rules carry an accent mark on the syllable to be stressed:
    táxi (*taxi*)

When Portuguese people speak fast they link words together and sometimes omit part of a word:
    p'ra instead of **para** (*to*)
    t'obrigado instead of **muito obrigado** (*thank you very much*)
So, whenever necessary, make the following request:
    Fale mais devagar, faz favor. (*Speak more slowly please.*)

Portuguese Pronunciation

Vowel sounds   *Practise saying these words*

a	when stressed, like *a* in h*a*t	fale (*speak*)
	when stressed before an **m** or **n**, and at the end of word, like *a* in *a*mong	cama (*bed*)
á, à	like *a* as in h*a*t	à (*at*)
â	like *a* in *a*mong	Alfândega (*Customs*)
	stressed, like *e* in t*e*ll	ela (*she*)
	stressed, in some cases, like *e* in th*e*y	ele (*he*)
	at the end of word and elsewhere, like *e* in butt*e*r	fale (*speak*)
é	like *e* in t*e*ll	café (*coffee*)
ê	like *e* in th*e*y	inglês (*English*)
	stressed, like *ee* in m*ee*t	dia (*day*)
	unstressed, like *i* in c*i*garette	cigarro (*cigarette*)
	like *ee* in m*ee*t	país (*country*)

o	stressed, like o in lot	posso (*may I*)
	stressed, in some cases, like o in note	Porto (*Oporto*)
	at the end of word and elsewhere	centro (*town centre*)
ó	like o in lot	próximo (*next*)
ô, ou	like o in note	vôo (*flight*)
		pouco (*little*)
u, ú	usually like oo in soon, but	tudo (*everything*)
		número (*number*)
	silent after **g** or **q** when an **e** or **i** follows	esquerda (*left*), seguir (*go on*)

Vowel groups

ai	like y in my	mais (*more*)
au	like ow in how	mau (*bad*)
ei	like ay in pay	direita (*right*)
eu	like e in they plus oo in soon	meu (*my, mine*)
oi	like o in note plus y in yet	dois (*two*)

Nasalised vowels

ã, am, an	like an in anchor	maçã (*apple*), ambos (*both*), banco (*bank*)
ão, am	(end of word) like ow in how, nasalised	não (*no*), desejam (*wish*)
ãe, em	(end of word) like ay in pay, nasalised	pães (*loaves*), em (*in, on*)
em, en	like e in they, nasalised	quente (*hot*), embarcar (*embark*)
êm	like ay in pay, nasalised and repeated	têm (*they have*)
im, in	like ee in meet, nasalised	sim (*yes*), cinco (*five*)
om, on	like o in note, nasalised	bom (*good*), onde (*where*)
õe	like o in note plus y in yet, nasalised	aviões (*aeroplanes*)
um, un	like oo in soon, nasalised	um (*one*), juntos (*together*)

Consonants

Most are similar to English, but remember to pronounce **p**, **t**, **c**, **b**, **d**, **g** more softly.

Also note the following:

c	like c in car before **a**, **o** and **u**, otherwise like s in so	com (*with*)
		cem (*a hundred*)
ç	like s in so	serviço (*service*)
ch	like sh in show	chave (*key*)
g	like g in go before **a**, **o** and **u**, but like s in pleasure before **e** and **i**	devagar (*slowly*)
		longe (*far*)
h	silent	hotel (*hotel*)
j	like s in pleasure	loja (*shop*)

lh	like *lli* in mi*lli*on	bilhete (*ticket*)
m, n	as in English when not nasalising a vowel (see Nasalised vowels)	mala (*suitcase*), nada (*nothing*)
nh	like *ni* in o*ni*on	vinho (*wine*)
r	at the beginning of word or syllable, like rolled Scottish *r*	rua (*road, street*)
	elsewhere, like *r* in ba*k*ery	caro (*expensive*)
rr	like rolled Scottish *r*	carro (*car*)
s	like *s* in *s*o, but like *z* in *z*one between vowels	sem (*without*) inglesa (*Englishwomen*)
	like *sh* in *sh*ow at the end of word or syllable in general	inglês (*Englishman*)
ss	like *s* in *s*o	passaporte (*passport*)
x	like *sh* in *sh*ow, at the beginning of word and in some cases between vowels	puxe (*pull*)
	like *s* in *s*o between vowels	próximo (*next*)
	like *z* in *z*one when *ex* comes before a vowel	exemplo (*example*)
z	like *z* in *z*one	zero (*zero*)
	like *sh* in *sh*ow at the end of word in general	faz (*do, does*)

Introduction to Portuguese Grammar

1   The
All nouns in Portuguese are either masculine or feminine and you should always learn each new word together with its gender.

The word for *the* with a masculine noun is **o**: **o** quarto (*the bedroom*); with a feminine noun is **a**: **a** cama (*the bed*); with a masculine noun in the plural is **os**: **os** quartos (*the bedrooms*); with a feminine noun in the plural is **as**: **as** camas (*the beds*). The noun itself may end in an **o** or an **a** according to its gender but not necessarily so: **o** quarto but **o** passaporte.

2   A/an, some, any
The word for *a/an* in Portuguese is **um** for a masculine noun: **um** mapa (*a map*); **uma** for a feminine noun: **uma** planta (*a streetmap*).

Unlike English, in Portuguese you do not need a word for *some* or *any* when asking for something:

Tem folhetos de informação? (*Do you have any brochures?*)

3 Adjectives

In Portuguese, the ending of adjectives depends on the nouns they accompany. Most adjectives end in **-o** with a masculine noun and change their ending to **-a** to accompany a feminine noun, but adjectives ending in **-e** do not change: **uma** cama pequen**a** (*the small bed*) but **uma** cama grande (*the large bed*). There are also some special cases: **um** quarto **bom** (*a good bedroom*), **uma** praia **boa** (*a good beach*). Adjectives in **-ês** for nationality change to **-esa** (See Pronunciation guide).

Like nouns, most adjectives in Portuguese add -s for plural:

Tem quartos vagos? (*Do you have any rooms free?*)

In general, adjectives in Portuguese follow the noun: um **hotel bom** (*a good hotel*). However, they come after the noun in some cases, for example when you express a wish: **Bom dia!** (*Good morning!*).

4 Of

De, meaning *of*, changes in form depending whether the noun that follows is masculine, feminine, singular or plural:

de + o = **do**; de + a = **da**; de + os = **dos**; de + as = **das**
Uma planta **da** cidade (*a streetmap of the town*); os passaportes **das** senhoras (*the ladies's passports*, literally, the passports of the ladies).

De, however, is invariable when used to describe a noun and in some expressions of quantity:

a mala **de** viagem (*the suitcase*); a mala **de** mão (*the handbag*); um cheque **de** viagem (*a traveller's cheque*); uma sanduíche **de** fiambre (*a ham sandwich*); uma garrafa **de** vinho (*a bottle of wine*); um pouco **de** leite (*a little milk*).

5 In and On

Em for *in* or *on* also changes form depending on the noun that follows:

em + o = **no**; em + a = **na**; em + os = **nos**; em + as = **nas**
no hotel (*in the hotel*); **na** praia (*on the beach*).

6 This, that

For *this* use **este** to accompany a masculine noun and **esta** to accompany a feminine noun:

este passaporte (*this passport*); **esta** mala de viagem (*this suitcase*).

If you do not know what gender the noun is, just say **isto** for *this*: **isto** é meu (*this is mine*). For *that* use **isso** for something that is not near you but is near the person you are talking to and **aquilo** for something 'over there', away from both you and the person you are talking to: **isso** é meu; **aquilo** é meu. (*that is mine*).

My, your

Although the use of possessives in this book is limited to *my, mine* and *your, yours*, the full list is as follows:

o meu/a minha	*my, mine*
o seu/a sua	*your, yours*
o/a dele/dela	*his/her, hers*
o nosso/a nossa	*our, ours*
o seu/a sua	*your, yours* (talking to more than one person)
o/a deles/delas	*their, theirs*

Note that **meu**, **seu** and **nosso** agree with the noun they refer to, but **dele(s)** and **dela(s)** agree with the person to whom the things belong:

O seu passaporte, faz favor.	*Your passport, please.*
Esta mala de viagem é **a minha**.	*This suitcase is mine.*
Este carro é **o dela**.	*This car is hers.*
É a bagagem **deles**.	*It is their luggage.*

When it is obvious to whom something belongs, the word for *my, your*, etc. is often omitted:

Perdi o passaporte.   *I've lost my passport.*

I, you, etc.

The full list is as follows:

eu	*I*
o senhor/a senhora	*you* (masc./fem.)
o + (*male name*)/a + (*female name*)	
ele	*he, it*
ela	*she, it*

nós	*we*
os senhores/as senhoras;	*you* (more than on
o + (*male names*)/a + (*female names*)	
eles	*they* (masc.)
elas	*they* (fem.)

When talking to strangers and acquaintances, you use **o senh** for a man and **a senhora** for a lady: Como está **a senhora**? (*H₀ are you?*); **O senhor** é inglês? (*Are you English?*).

Note the following: **Os senhores** são ingleses? (*Are y₀ English?*) addressing a man and a woman at the same time.

When talking to a friend, you use the person's name: Con está **o João**? (*How are you?*) talking to John. **O João** e **a Tere** estão bem? (*Are you well?*) talking to John and Teresa.

Alternatively, you can leave '*you*' out and simply say **Con está**? (*How are you?*) whether talking to a stranger, your frie₁ João or anyone else. If you are talking to more than one perso just say: **Como estão**? (*How are you?*).

In actual fact, the words for *I*, *you*, etc. are often left out: **Est₀ bem** (*I am well*) instead of **Eu estou bem** (*I am well*).

9 Verbs

(*a*) Most Portuguese verbs fall into one of three categorie ending in either **-ar**, **-er** or **-ir**. Here are examples of verbs these categories:

desejar *to wish, to want*

eu	desej**o**	nós	desej**amos**
o sr./a sra.; etc.	desej**a**	os srs./as sras.; etc.	desej**am**
ele/ela	desej**a**	eles/elas	desej**am**

Que desej**a**? *What do you wish?* the waiter asks you (English *What would you like?/May I he you?*)

Desej**o** ... *I'd like* ...

vender *to sell*

eu	vend**o**	nós	vend**emos**
o sr./a sra.; etc.	vend**e**	os srs./as sras.; etc.	vend**em**
ele/ela	vend**e**	eles/elas	vend**em**

Vend**e** jornais ingleses? *Do you sell English newspaper*

partir *to leave, depart*

eu	part**o**	nós	part**imos**

| o sr./a sra.; etc. | parte | os srs./as sras.; etc. | partem |
| ele/ela | parte | eles/elas | partem |

Partimos amanhã. *We are leaving tomorrow.*

(*b*) There are, however, irregular verbs in Portuguese. They have to be learnt as you go along. Here are some of the more common ones which are used in this book:

ser (*to be*):	eu **sou**, o sr. **é**, ele **é**, nós **somos**, os srs. **são**, eles **são**. Sou inglês. *I am English.* Onde é a farmácia? *Where is the chemist's?*
estar (*to be*, for temporary conditions and for location of movables):	eu **estou**, o sr. **está**, ele **está**, nós **estamos**, os srs. **estão**, eles **estão**. Está bem! *It's OK!* Estou aqui em férias. *I am here on holiday.* Onde está o carro? *Where is the car?*
ter (*to have*):	eu **tenho**, o sr. **tem**, ele **tem**, nós **temos**, os srs. **têm**, eles **têm**. Tem uma planta de Lisboa? *Do you have a streetmap of Lisbon?*
poder (*can, may*):	eu **posso**, o sr. **pode**, ele **pode**, nós **podemos**, os srs. **podem**, eles **podem**. Posso? *May I?*
saber (*to know*):	eu **sei**, o sr. **sabe**, ele **sabe**, nós **sabemos**, os srs. **sabem**, eles **sabem**. Não sei. *I don't know.*
ir (*to go*):	eu **vou**, o sr. **vai**, ele **vai**, nós **vamos**, os srs. **vão**, eles **vão**. Vamos para a praia. *We are going to the beach.*
fazer (*to do, make*):	eu **faço**, o sr. **faz**, ele **faz**, nós **fazemos**, os srs. **fazem**, eles **fazem**. Vamos fazer uma excursão. *We're going on a outing (to make an excursion).*

Note the use of **fazer** with expressions of politeness:
    Faz favor! *Excuse me, please!* (to draw someone's attention).

Uma sanduíche, faz favor. *A sandwich, please.* (to ask for something).

Also note the use of **fazer** with expressions concerning the weather:

Faz bom tempo. *The weather is good.*

(*c*) Many of the verbs in this book are in the 'Polite Imperative' which is a form often used for making requests or giving orders:

Fale devagar, faz favor.   *Speak slowly, please.*
Vire à direita.   *Turn right.*
Siga.   *Go./Drive.*
Pare!   *Stop!*

(*d*) Saying *No*.
The word **não** is used for *no* and also for *not*.
Note that **não** (=*not*) comes before the verb.

Não. *No.*
Não compreendo. *I don't understand.*

(*e*) Asking questions.
Often you just raise your voice at the end of a sentence:

Esta mala de viagem é a sua. *This suitcase is yours.*
Esta mala de viagem é a sua? *Is this suitcase yours?*

When you start with a question-word (**Onde**, *Where*; **Quanto**, *How much*; etc.) the verb is inverted:

Onde é o hotel? *Where is the hotel?*
Quanto é o quarto? *How much is the room?*

Also, instead of inverting the verb, **é que** can be used:

Onde é que o hotel é? *Where is the hotel?*

General Expressions

Yes, No **b.** Hello, Goodbye **c.** Please, Thank
u **d.** Mr, Mrs **e.** The, This **f.** I, My . . .

sim	*yes*
não	*no*

Tudo bem?	*Everything O.K.?*
Sim, tudo bem.	*Yes, everything O.K.*

bom dia	*hello/goodbye* (between daybreak and noon)
boa tarde	*hello/goodbye* (between noon and sunset)
boa noite	*hello/goodbye* (between sunset and daybreak)
o senhor	*you* (to a man)
a senhora	*you* (to a woman)

Boa tarde!	*Hello! Good afternoon.*
Como está a senhora?	*How are you?*
Estou bem, e o senhor?	*I am well, and you?*
Muito bem.	*Very well.*
Boa noite.	*Goodbye. Good night.*
Até à próxima.	*See you again.*

c. | | |
|---|---|
| **faz favor (f.f.)** | *please; excuse me, please* |
| **com licença** | *excuse me* (literally *with your permission*) |
| **obrigado** | *thank you* (said by male) |
| **obrigada** | *thank you* (said by female) |
| **desculpe** | *pardon me, sorry* |

O seu passaporte, f.f..	*Your passport, please.*
Muito obrigado.	*Thank you very much.*
Muito obrigada.	*Thank you very much.*
De nada.	*Not at all.*
Com licença!	*Excuse me!* (you want to get through)
Faz favor!	*Excuse me, please!* (to draw someone's attention)
Posso?	*May I?*

d. | | |
|---|---|
| **o senhor (Sr.)** | *gentleman (Mr)* |
| **a senhora (Srª. Dona)** | *lady (Mrs/Miss/Ms)* |
| **o menino, a menina** | *boy, girl* |

A senhora é a Srª. Dona Rita Lourenço?	*Are you Ms Rita Lourenço?*

e. | | |
|---|---|
| **o** (m), **a** (f) | *the* (singular) |
| **os** (m), **as** (f) | *the* (plural) |
| **um** (m), **uma** (f) | *a/an* |
| **este** (m), **esta** (f) | *this* |

A mala de viagem.	*The suitcase.*
Esta mala de viagem.	*This suitcase.*

f. | | |
|---|---|
| **eu** | *I* |
| **o meu** (m), **a minha** (f) | *my/mine* |
| **o seu** (m), **a sua** (f) | *your/yours* |

O seu nome, f.f..	*Your name, please.*
Aqui tem a sua chave.	*Here's your key.*
Esta mala de viagem é a sua?	*Is this suitcase yours?*
É o meu marido.	*This is my husband.*
É a minha mulher.	*This is my wife.*
Muito prazer.	*Pleased to meet you.*

1   General Expressions

1   You are John Evans. You are asked: **O senhor é o Sr. John Evans?** What do you answer?

2   You are Jean White. You are asked: **A senhora é a Sr². Dona Sarah Williams?** What do you answer?

3   You want to greet a Portuguese. It is around 10.00 am. What do you say?

4   How do you say *How are you?* to a lady?

5   You want to say *Goodbye*. It is around 4.00 pm. What do you say?

6   You want to say *See you again*. What do you say?

7   What do you say to draw someone's attention?

8   How do you say *Thank you*?

9   When someone thanks you, what do you reply?

10   There is a long queue of people and you want to get through. What do you say?

11   You bump into someone. What do you say?

12   How do you say *This suitcase is mine*?

13   Mr Andrews would like to introduce his wife. What does he say?

14   Mrs Andrews would like to introduce her husband. What does she say?

15   You have been introduced to a Portuguese. What do you say?

16   You are introducing yourself. How do you say *My name is . . .*?

Portuguese people usually shake hands each time they meet and also when saying goodbye.

When you have made friends, you can use the word **Olá**, preferably with the person's name: **Olá João! Bom dia!** *Hi John! Hello!*. Also, you can add **Adeus** to your parting words: **Adeus! Boa noite.** *Bye-bye.*

With your friends it will be suitable to replace the word **o senhor/a senhora** (= *you*) with the person's name: **Como está a Teresa?** *How are you?* (talking to Teresa).

Here are some useful words and expressions

É ...	*It is ...*	um pouco	*a little*
bom	*good*	muito	*a lot*
mau	*bad*	com	*with*
grande	*big*	sem	*without*
pequeno	*small*	perto	*near*
fácil	*easy*	longe	*far*
difícil	*difficult*		
pesado	*heavy*	**Está ...**	*It is ...*
leve	*light*	com	*with*
caro	*expensive*	sem	*without*
barato	*cheap*		
cedo	*early*		
tarde	*late*	perto	*near*

(for a person, referring to company)

		longe	*far*
		aberto	*open*
		fechado	*closed*

com *with* / sem *without* (for a person, referring to company)

perto *near* / longe *far* / aberto *open* / fechado *closed* (for a person, car or anything else that can move about)

Arriving in Portugal

a. Customs **b.** Documents **c.** Nationality

a	**alfândega**	*customs*
	declarar	*declare*
a	**bagagem**	*luggage*
o	**porta-bagagem**	*boot* (of a car)
a	**mala de viagem**	*suitcase*
a	**mala de mão**	*handbag*
o	**saco**	*bag, carrier-bag*

Tem alguma coisa a declarar?	*Do you have anything to declare?*
Não, nada a declarar.	*No, nothing to declare.*
Esta é a sua bagagem?	*Is this your luggage?*
Abra a sua mala, faz favor.	*Open your case, please.*
Abra o porta-bagagem.	*Open the boot.*
É para uso pessoal.	*It is for my personal use.*
Está bem. Pode seguir.	*It's O.K. You may go on.*

o	**passaporte**	*passport*
a	**carta de condução**	*driving-licence*

os	**documentos do carro**	*car registration-papers*
o	**nome**	*name*
o	**nome próprio**	*first name*
o	**apelido,** o **nome de família**	*surname*
a	**residência**	*place of residence*

O seu passaporte, faz favor.	*Your passport, please.*
Como é o seu nome? =Como se chama?	*What is your name?*
O meu nome é . . . =Chamo-me . . .	*My name is . . .*
Está aqui em viagem de negócios?	*Are you here on business?*
Não, estou aqui em férias.	*No, I am here on holiday.*

c.

a	**nacionalidade**	*nationality*
	Portugal	*Portugal*
o	**português**	*Portuguese man*
a	**portuguesa**	*Portuguese woman*
	português/portuguesa	*Portuguese*
a	**Grã-Bretanha**	*Great Britain*
	britânico/britânica	*British*
a	**Inglaterra**	*England*
o	**inglês**	*Englishman*
a	**inglesa**	*Englishwoman*
	inglês/inglesa	*English*
a	**Escócia**	*Scotland*
	escocês/escocesa	*Scottish*
o	**País de Gales**	*Wales*
	galês/galesa	*Welsh*
a	**Irlanda (do Norte)**	*(Northern) Ireland*
	irlandês/irlandesa	*Irish*
a	**embaixada**	*embassy*
o	**consulado**	*consulate*

O senhor é inglês?	*Are you English?*
Sim, sou inglês.	*Yes, I'm English.*
Não compreendo.	*I don't understand.*
Fale mais devagar, f.f..	*Speak more slowly, please.*
Fale inglês?	*Do you speak English?*
Tem um jornal inglês?	*Do you have an English newspaper?*

2   Arriving in Portugal

What are these called in Portuguese?

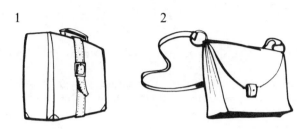

1

2

3   What does the customs official ask you?

4   You have nothing to declare. What do you answer?

5   The customs official would like you to open your suitcase. What does he say?

6   The customs official is satisfied. What does he say?

7   The passport control official would like to see your passport. What does he say to you?

8   You are arriving by car. The border guard would like to see your driving licence. What does he say?

9   The border guard asks you your name. What do you say?

10 You are asked whether you are visiting the country on business. You are on holiday. What do you say?

11 Mr Johnson is asked: **O senhor é inglês?** What does he answer?

12 Mrs McClelland is asked: **A senhora é inglesa?** What does she answer?

13 Explain in Portuguese what the following letters stand for.

14 What do you say when you don't understand?

15 You would like to buy an English newspaper. How do you ask the shopkeeper whether he has got any?

– You are advised to check on customs allowances and purchase of duty-free goods before setting out on your trip.
– The address of the **Portuguese National Tourist Office** in London is:

  1/5 New Bond Street, London W1Y ONP Tel: (01) 493 3873

– If you are going to Portugal by car, you must be in possession of a British or International driving licence, the car registration document, the 'Green Card' insurance and nationality plates or stickers. If you are taking a car which is not registered in your name, you must have a letter of authority from the owner which should be officially recognised by the Portuguese Consulate General.
– It is advisable to carry a spare parts kit and beam deflectors.
– Portuguese frontier posts are usually open between 7 am and midnight, but close earlier in winter. In summer some are open 24 hours.
– The address of the **United Kingdom Embassy** and Consulate in Lisbon is:

  Rua São Domingos à Lapa, 37, Lisboa 1200 Tel: 66 11 91

  The Consulate in Oporto is at the following address:

  Avenida da Boa Vista 3072, Oporto

Driving a Car

Vehicles **b.** Roads **c.** Service Stations
Parking.

o	**carro**	*car*
a	**caravana**	*caravan*
o	**camião**	*lorry*
	Veículos Pesados	*Heavy Vehicles*
o	**trânsito**	*traffic*
	siga	*go, drive*

A luguer de carros.	*Car rental.*
Vamos para Lisboa.	*Let's go to Lisbon.*

b.

a	**estrada**	*road*
a	**auto-estrada**	*motorway*
a	**portagem**	*toll*
	Desvio	*Diversion*
	Obras, Trabalhos	*Road Works*
	Cuidado, Atenção	*Caution*
	Perigo	*Danger*
	Prioridade	*Right of Way*
	Reduzir Marcha	*Slow Down*
	Pare	*Stop*

A estrada nacional (N)	*Major road.*
A estrada de Lisboa.	*The road to Lisbon.*
Boa viagem!	*Have a good journey!*

c.

a	**bomba de gasolina**	*filling station*
a	**gasolina**	*petrol*
o	**gasóleo**	*diesel*
o	**óleo**	*oil*
a	**água**	*water*
os	**pneus**	*tyres*

Super? Normal?	*4 star? 2 star?*
Quanto?	*How much?*
Vinte litros, f.f..	*Twenty litres, please.*
Encha.	*Fill it up.*
Verifique o óleo, f.f..	*Check the oil, please.*

d.

o	**estacionamento, o parqueamento**	*parking, car park*
o	**parcómetro**	*parking meter*
a	**garagem**	*garage*

Estacionamento proibido.	*No parking.*
Paragem proibida.	*No waiting.*

Numbers→7, Breakdowns, Accidents→20

3 Driving a Car

What are these called in Portuguese?

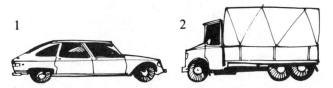

3 The petrol station attendant wants to know whether you would like 4-star or 2-star petrol. What does he ask you?

4 How do you ask the attendant to fill it up?

5 How do you ask him to check the oil and the tyres?

6 He wishes you a good journey. What does he say?

Explain in Portuguese what the following traffic signs mean:

- **Traffic rules:** In Portugal the rule of the road is drive on the right. Priority is given to vehicles coming from the right, in general. In general, overtake on the left, but overtake a stationary tram on the right and at moderate speed. At a tram stop, overtaking is forbidden when passengers are entering or leaving a tram.

- **Speed limits:** The maximum in built-up areas is 60 kilometres per hour (37 mph) for cars and 50 kph (30 mph) for cars with trailers. Outside towns the maximum speed limit is 90 kph (55 mph) for cars and 70 kph (40 mph) for cars with trailers. On motorways the minimum and maximum speed limits are respectively 40 kph (26 mph) and 120 kph (75 mph).

- **Parking:** Vehicles must be parked facing in the same direction as traffic moving on that side of the road, except in special cases. In Blue Zone districts free discs are obtainable from the local police and from the Portuguese Automobile Club (ACP), Rua Rosa Araújo, 24, Lisboa.

  A red warning triangle should be carried. If you are forced to stop in moving traffic, through breakdown or other reason, and your vehicle is not visible from a distance of 100 metres (110 yards), place the triangle at no less than 30 metres (35 yards) behind it.

- **Car hire:** Self-drive and chauffeur-driven cars are widely available and operated by local and international firms. The minimum age for self-drive car rental is 23. Current UK licences are valid.

- **Petrol:** Petrol is sold by the litre (1 gallon = 4.54 litres). It is available in two grades, 4-Star (**super**) and 2-Star (**normal**). These can be mixed to obtain 3-Star grade.

Finding Your Way

Maps **b.** In Town **c.** Streets
Directions

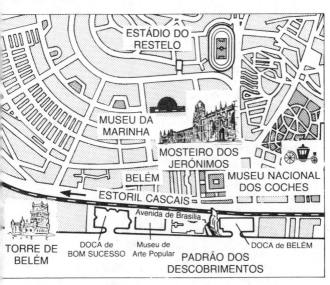

| o | **mapa** | *map* |
| a | **planta** | *street map* |

| Tem um mapa das estradas? | *Do you have a road map?* |
| Uma planta de Lisboa, f.f.. | *A street map of Lisbon, please.* |

a	**cidade**	*city, town*
o	**centro**	*city/town centre*
o	**município**	*town hall*
a	**casa**	*house*
a	**vila**	*small town*
a	**aldeia**	*village*

| A cidade de Lisboa. | *The city of Lisbon.* |
| Fazer uma volta turística (da cidade). | *Go on a sightseeing tour (of the city).* |

c.

a	**rua**	*street, urban road*
a	**avenida**	*avenue*
o	**largo**	*square*
a	**praça**	*square*
a	**zona de peões**	*pedestrian zone*
o	**semáforo**	*traffic lights*
	Sentido Único	*One-Way Street*
	onde fica . . .?	*where is . . .?*

Onde fica a Praça Marquês de Pombal?	*Where is the Marquês de Pombal Square?*
Onde é que o senhor está hospedado?	*Where are you staying? (asking a man)*
Estou hospedado no Hotel Central.	*I am staying in Hotel Central.*
Onde é que a senhora está hospedada	*Where are you staying? (asking a lady)*

d.

o	**caminho**	*way, direction*
a	**curva**	*bend*
	vire	*turn*
	à esquerda	*(to the) left*
	à direita	*(to the) right*
	em frente	*straight ahead*
o	**norte**	*north*
o	**sul**	*south*
o	**este,** o **leste**	*east*
o	**oeste**	*west*

Qual é o caminho para a ponte, f.f.?	*Which way to the bridge, please?*
Faz favor, vou bem para a Torre de Belém?	*Excuse me, please, am I on the right road for the Tower of Belém?*
Siga em frente.	*Go straight ahead.*
Vire à direita.	*Turn right.*
É longe?	*Is it far?*
Não, é muito perto.	*No, it's quite near.*

Numbers→7, Places of Interest→15, Excursions→16

Finding Your Way

1 What does each letter stand for in Portuguese?

2 You want to buy a street map of Lisbon. What do you say?

3 You want to buy a road map. How do you ask whether the shopkeeper has got one?

4 You don't know where Praça Marquês de Pombal is. How do you ask a passer-by?

5 You want to know the direction to Belém. What do you say?

6 How do you tell someone to turn right?

7 How do you tell someone to turn left?

8 How do you tell someone to go straight on?

9 You want to know whether it is far. What do you say?

0 Say the names of the following Portuguese cities and towns: Lisboa, Porto, Coimbra, Setúbal, Braga, Sintra, Nazaré, Évora, Faro, Sagres, Albufeira, Guimarães.

11 You want to go to the east side of Lisbon. Which lane do you get into?

- **Maps,** town plans, lists of hotels and other useful information can be obtained from the local tourist offices. They are usually open on weekdays from 9 am to 7 pm. Some close on Sundays and public holidays.

- The different kinds of roads in Portugal are:
  Auto-estrada (motorway, expressway); **Estrada Principal/Tráfico Internacional** (major road/international traffic); the older name **Estrada Nacional** (major road); **Estrada Secundária** (secondary road); **Estrada Municipal** (municipal road).

- Here are some useful **road signs**:
  sentido único – one-way road
  seguir pela direita/esquerda – keep right/left
  travessia de peões – pedestrian crossing
  pare, olhe, escute – stop, look, listen

- Pedestrians do not necessarily have right of way at zebra crossings.

Public Transport

Railways **b.** Aeroplanes **c.** Ships
Public Transport **e.** Information

os	**caminhos de ferro**	*railways*
a	**estação**	*railway station*
	Depósito de bagagem	*left luggage office*
	Cacifos	*left luggage lockers*
a	**bilheteira**	*ticket office*
o	**bilhete**	*ticket*
a	**reserva**	*reservation*
a	**linha, a via**	*track, platform*
o	**comboio**	*train*
o	**rápido**	*fast train*
o	**expresso**	*express train*
	Vagão-restaurante	*dining car*
	Carruagem-cama	*sleeping car*
a	**sala de espera**	*waiting room*

A Estação de Santa Apolónia.	*Santa Apolónia Station. (Lisbon).*
Um bilhete de segunda classe para o Porto, f.f..	*A second-class ticket to Oporto, please.*
Um bilhete de ida e volta.	*A return ticket.*
Linha 3 (três).	*Platform 3.*

b.
o	**aeroporto**	*airport*
o	**avião**	*aeroplane*
o	**vôo**	*flight*

c.
o	**porto**	*port*
a	**gare marítima**	*embarkment area*
o	**barco**	*boat/ship*
a	**coberta**	*deck*
o	**camarote**	*cabin*

> Onde é a marina?   *Where is the marina?*

d.
o	**metro**	*underground train*
	Correspondência	*connections*
	Saída	*exit*
o	**autocarro**	*bus*
a	**paragem de autocarro**	*bus-stop*
o	**eléctrico**	*tram*
a	**camioneta**	*coach*
o	**táxi**	*taxi*
a	**praça de táxis**	*taxi rank*
	Livre	*free, for hire*

> Onde é a estação do metro?   *Where is the underground station?*
> Uma caderneta, f.f..   *A book of tickets, please.*
> Chame-me um táxi, f.f..   *Get me a taxi, please.*
> Para a Estação do Cais do Sodré, f.f..   *To the Cais do Sodré Station, please.*

e.
a	**informação**	*information*
	Informações	*Information desk*
o	**horário**	*timetable*
	Partida(s)	*Departure(s)*
	Chegada(s)	*Arrival(s)*
o	**atraso**	*delay*

Customs→2, Numbers→7, Times→8, Money→9

What sign do you look for at the railway station
1   if you need information?

2   if you want to leave your luggage in a locker?

3 if you want to buy a ticket?

4 How do you ask for a return ticket to Coimbra?

5 You would like to have lunch in the train. Which carriage do you look for?

6 You want to sleep during the train journey. Which carriage do you travel in?

7 You want to go to the airport. What do you say to the taxi-driver?

8 You arrive at the airport and want Departures. What sign do you look for?

9 You want to know where the bus-stop is. What do you ask?

What sign do you look for in the Lisbon underground

0 if you want to change trains?

11 if you want to leave the station?

12 You are at the ticket window. How do you ask for a
    book of tickets?

– **LAR air services** operate domestic flights between
  Lisbon, Oporto, Faro and other towns. In Madeira
  there are scheduled TAP flights between Funchal and
  Porto Santo, and in the Azores SATA operate inter-
  island flights.

– **Portuguese Railways** provides a network of services
  throughout the country as well as international services.
  Express and fast trains connect Lisbon and Oporto at
  frequent intervals. There are direct night trains connect-
  ing Oporto, Lisbon and the Algarve which provide
  sleeping and car-carrying facilities.

  Reduced rates are available in the form of tourist
  tickets, family tickets, group tickets and kilometric
  tickets. Children under the age of 4 travel free and
  between 4 and 12 pay half fare. There is a 50% fare
  reduction for senior citizens (over 65).

– **Coach Services** cover the country and timetables are
  available from local tourist offices and travel agencies in
  Portugal.

– **Urban transport:** For Lisbon city buses and trams you
  can save money by buying a swatch of tickets valid on
  both. The cable car (**o elevador** or **o ascensor**) is an
  alternative to the tram for climbing some of the steepest
  hills of Lisbon. Oporto is served by trams, buses and
  trolley-buses. Tickets at reduced prices are available.

  Lisbon underground electric trains are also a cheap
  and convenient way of travelling. There is a standard
  fare for any single journey. For several journeys, it
  works out cheaper to buy a book of tickets. A large red
  M (for Metro) marks the entrance to an underground
  train station.

  Taxis are painted black with green roofs. They are
  only allowed to pick up from ranks.

  In Lisbon, there is also a ferry service across the river
  Tagus from several quays such as Praça do Comércio,
  Cais do Sodré and Belém.

a. Hotels, Camping   **b.** Hotel Rooms
c. Prices   **d.** Toilets

a.

o	**hotel**	*hotel*
o	**motel**	*motel*
a	**pensão**	*guesthouse*
o	**parque de campismo**	*campsite*
a	**pousada de juventude**	*youth hostel*
a	**pousada, estalagem**	*inn*

Há um hotel aqui perto?	*Is there a hotel nearby?*
Um hotel bom.	*A good hotel.*
Onde é o parque de campismo?	*Where is the campsite?*

b.

a	**recepção**	*reception*
o	**quarto**	*room*
a	**cama**	*bed*

o	**chuveiro**	*shower*
a	**casa de banho**	*bathroom*
a	**chave**	*key*
o	**rés-do-chão (R/C)**	*ground floor*
o	**andar**	*floor (storey)*
a	**escada**	*stairs*
o	**ascensor, elevador**	*lift*

Tem um quarto vago?	*Do you have a room free?*
Reservei um quarto duplo.	*I booked a double room.*
Um quarto para uma noite.	*A room for one night.*
Um quarto com duas camas.	*A room with two beds.*
Com chuveiro e WC.	*With shower and toilet.*
O hotel está cheio.	*The hotel is full booked.*
A minha chave, f.f..	*My key, please.*
O número do seu quarto?	*Your room number?*

c.	o **preço**	*price*
	caro	*expensive*
	a **conta**	*bill*
	a **pensão completa**	*full board*
	a **meia pensão**	*half board*

Quanto é o quarto?	*How much is the room?*
Qual é o preço com pequeno almoço?	*How much is it with breakfast?*
É muito caro.	*It's too expensive.*
Quero pagar agora.	*I want to pay now.*
Aqui tem a sua conta.	*Here's your bill.*

d.	os **toiletes. os WC**	*toilets*
	Homens, Senhores, Cavalheiros	*Gentlemen*
	Mulheres, Senhoras	*Ladies*
	ocupado	*engaged*
	livre	*vacant*

Onde são os toiletes?	*Where are the toilets?*
Lá em baixo, à esquerda.	*Downstairs, on the left.*

Customs→2, Parking→3, Money→9, Meals→10

6   Accommodation

What are these called in Portuguese?

1

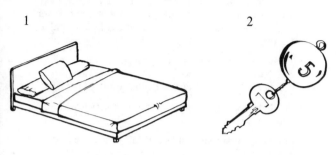

2

3   You're looking for a good hotel. What do you say to a passerby?

4   How do you ask at the reception desk whether they have a vacant room?

5   You want a room with shower for one night. What do you say?

6   Ask how much the room costs with breakfast.

7   Say that you find it too expensive.

8   Say that you want to pay.

9   What do the letters below in a lift stand for in Portuguese?

10   You want to know where the toilets are. What do you say?

11   What does the sign say if the toilet is vacant?

12   What does it say if the toilet is engaged?

- **Hotel accommodation** ranges from five-star luxury hotels to guest-houses (**a pensão**). **Pousadas** are Government owned inns, often converted castles and palaces. **Estalagem** is the name given to a privately-run inn.

- **Manor and farm houses:** Many are set in states which are still farmed today and give you the opportunity of a holiday in direct contact with the countryside.

- **Youth hostels** offer accommodation at very low rates for young tourists.

- **Camping/caravanning** sites exist all over the country. It is advisable to have a Camping Carnet.

- **Villas,** apartments and studio flats are available if you prefer a self catering holiday.

- **Electricity:** In general, 220v AC with continental two pin plugs.

- **Toilets** can be signposted in a variety of ways: **Toiletes, WC, Retretes, Lavabos, Sanitários, Instalações Sanitárias**. Also there is a tendency euphemistically to use the name **casa de banho**:
  Onde é a casa de banho? = Onde são os toiletes? to ask for the toilet.

7 Numbers, Weights and Measures

a. Numbers b. Weights and Measures

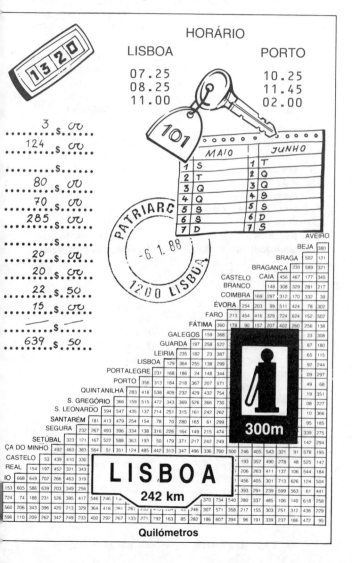

a.

0	zero	10	dez	20	vinte
1	um(m), uma(f)	11	onze	21	vinte e um, uma
2	dois(m), duas(f)	12	doze	22	vinte e dois, duas
3	três	13	treze	23	vinte e três
4	quatro	14	catorze	30	trinta
5	cinco	15	quinze	31	trinta e um, uma
6	seis	16	dezasseis	32	trinta e dois, duas
7	sete	17	dezassete	33	trinta e três
8	oito	18	dezoito	40	quarenta
9	nove	19	dezanove	50	cinquenta

60	sessenta	500	quinhentos
70	setenta	600	seiscentos
80	oitenta	700	setecentos
90	noventa	800	oitocentos
100	cem	900	novecentos
101	cento e um, uma	1 000	mil
125	cento e vinte e cinco	2 000	dois mil, duas mil
200	duzentos	100 000	cem mil
300	trezentos	1 000 000	um milhão
400	quatrocentos	2 000 000	dois milhões

b.

o	**grama**	*gram*
o	**quilo**	*kilogram*
o	**litro**	*litre*
o	**metro**	*metre*
o	**quilómetro**	*kilometre*
o	**centímetro**	*centimetre*
	quanto . . .?	*how much . . .?*
	um pouco	*a little*
	muito	*a lot*

Duzentos gramas de manteiga.	*200 grams of butter.*
Quanto de uvas?	*How many grapes?*
Um quilo de uvas, f.f..	*A kilo of grapes, please.*
Um pouco de leite.	*A little milk.*
Cem quilómetros até Faro.	*A hundred kilometres to Faro.*

Times and Dates→8, Money and Shopping→9

Which platform do these trains leave from?

HORÁRIO		Linha
Cascais	21.15	5
Estoril	21.25	3
Algés	21.30	4

1 The train to Cascais.

2 The train to Estoril.

3 The train to Algés.

What are the numbers of the rooms these people are staying in?

4 Sr. Lourenço

5 Sr. Magalhães

6 Mr Thompson

7 Mr Williams

8 Where does Sr. Magalhães live? Read out his address in Portuguese.

> Rua da República, 87
> 1500 Lisboa

9 What is Sr. Magalhães's telephone number? Read it out in Portuguese.

> 53 22 01

Read out the following distances in Portuguese:

10	Lisboa–Sagres	279 km
11	Lisboa–Albufeira	318 km
12	Lisboa–Faro	282 km
13	Lisboa–Monte Gordo	305 km

14 How much does this packet of butter weigh?

15 How much coffee is in this packet?

16 You want to buy a litre of milk. What do you say?

– In Portugal, the **metric system** of weights and measures is used:

kilograms		pounds	grams		ounces
1	=	2.2	100	=	3.5
5	=	11.0	250	=	9.0
litres		**gallons**	**kilometres**		**miles**
1	=	.22	1	=	.62
5	=	1.1	20	=	12.4

NB 1 lb = 0.45 kg; 1 pint = 0.57 litres;
1 gal. = 4.54 litres; 1 mile = 1.6 km; 8 km = 5 miles.

Times and Dates

Telling the Time   **b.** Times of the Day
Week and Month

o	**relógio**	*watch, clock*
a	**hora (h)**	*hour*
o	**minuto**	*minute*
o	**momento**	*moment*

Que horas são?	*What's the time?*
É uma hora.	*It's 1 o'clock.*
São dez horas da manhã.	*It's 10 o'clock in the morning.*
São dez horas e um quarto.	*It's a quarter past 10.*
São dez horas e meia.	*It's half past 10.*
São onze horas menos um quarto.	*It's a quarter to 11.*
São duas horas da tarde.	*It's 2 in the afternoon.*
Às nove horas da noite.	*At 9 o'clock at night.*
Às vinte e duas horas.	*At 10 pm.*

Uma hora.	*One hour.*
Uma meia-hora.	*Half an hour.*
Um quarto d'hora.	*A quarter of an hour.*
Um momento, f.f..	*Just a moment, please.*

b.

o	**dia**	*day*
a	**manhã**	*morning*
	meio dia	*noon*
a	**tarde**	*afternoon/early evening*
a	**noite**	*late evening/night*
	meia noite	*midnight*
	hoje	*today*
	amanhã	*tomorrow*
	ontem	*yesterday*
	todos os dias	*every day*

Quando é que o senhor parte?	*When are you leaving?*
Amanhã de manhã.	*Tomorrow morning.*
Amanhã à tarde, às 3 horas.	*Tomorrow afternoon, at 3 o'clock.*
Hoje à noite, às 9 horas.	*Tonight, at 9 o'clock.*
A que horas parte o avião?	*When does the plane leave?*
Ao meio dia.	*At midday*

c.

a	**semana**	*week*
	domingo	*Sunday*
	segunda-feira (2ªf.)	*Monday*
	terça-feira (3ªf.)	*Tuesday*
	quarta-feira (4ªf.)	*Wednesday*
	quinta-feira (5ªf.)	*Thursday*
	sexta-feira (6ªf.)	*Friday*
	sábado	*Saturday*
o	**mês, os meses**	*month, months*
o	**ano**	*year*

A próxima semana.	*Next week.*
A semana passada.	*Last week.*
Fechado à terça-feira.	*Closed on Tuesdays.*
Terça-feira, um de Julho.	*Tuesday, July 1st.*
5ªf., 22 de Agosto.	*Thursday, August 22nd.*

Public Transport→5, Numbers→7

Times and Dates

1 You want to know what time it is. What do you say?

2 Say what time of the morning it is for each of the clocks below.

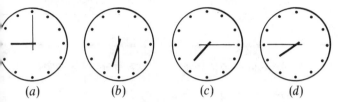

    (a)   (b)   (c)   (d)

3 *How do you say in Portuguese:* (a) 20 minutes; (b) 10 days; (c) 2 weeks; (d) 2 months.

4 The hotel desk clerk wants to know when Mrs Baker is leaving. What does he ask?

5 You are asked when you are leaving. Say that it is tomorrow night.

6 You want to know at what time the plane leaves. What do you ask?

BANCO

Horas de Abertura

Manhã : Das 8h 30 ao meio dia.

Tarde: Da 1h às 2h 30.

---

7 What are the opening times of the bank? Say them aloud.

8 Between what hours is there no parking?

9   On working days, how long can you park?

Partida do Porto	Chegada a Lisboa
20.15	23.15

10   At what time does this train leave from Oporto?

11   At what time does it arrive in Lisbon?

Quinta-Feira, 3 de Dezembro

12   When was this newspaper published?

> – The **months** of the year are: **Janeiro**, **Fevereiro**, **Março**,
> **Abril**, **Maio**, **Junho**, **Julho**, **Agosto**, **Setembro**, **Outubro**,
> **Novembro**, **Dezembro**.
>   Both months and days of the week may be written
> with either initial capital letters or lower-case letters.
>   Note that **Sábado** = on Saturday, and **ao Sábado**, **ao**
> **Domingo**, **à Segunda-Feira**, etc. = on Saturdays, Sun-
> days, Mondays, etc.
>   Unlike in English, years are not read in hundreds.
> 1995 = **mil**, **novecentos e noventa e cinco**.
> – The **24-hour clock** is used for official purposes (on
> timetables, etc.): 13.00 = 1 pm; 19.45 = 7.45 pm, and so
> on.

Money and Shopping

. Money   **b.** At the Bank, Changing Money
. Shopping   **d.** Paying

o **dinheiro**	*money*
o **troco**	*small change*
a **nota**	*note*
a **moeda**	*coin*
o **escudo ($)**	*escudo*
o **centavo**	*cent*

50 escudos (50$00), f.f..	*50 escudos, please.*
50 centavos.	*50 cents.*

o **banco**	*bank*
o **câmbio**	*currency exchange*
cambiar	*exchange*
o **cheque de viagem**	*traveller's cheque*
o **cartão de crédito**	*credit-card*

Desejo cambiar 50 libras.	*I'd like to change £50.*
Desejo cobrar este cheque de viagem.	*I'd like to cash this traveller's cheque.*

c.

	comprar	*to buy*
a	loja	*shop*
o	armazém	*department store*
o	supermercado	*supermarket*
o	mercado	*market*
	Auto-serviço	*Self-service*

Que deseja?	*May I help you?*
Estou só a ver.	*I'm just looking.*
Desejo . . .	*I'd like . . .*
Desejo uma T-shirt.	*I'd like a T-shirt.*
Tem T-shirts?	*Do you have any T-shirts?*
Mais alguma coisa?	*Anything else?*
Muito obrigado/obrigada.	*Thank you very much.*

d.

	preço	*price*
	pagar	*to pay*
a	caixa	*cash-desk*
	caro	*expensive*
	barato	*cheap*
	gratuito, grátis	*free*

Quanto é?	*How much is it?*
São 100 escudos.	*It's 100 escudos.*
É muito caro.	*It's too expensive.*
Quanto é tudo?	*How much does it come to?*
Pague na caixa, f.f..	*Please pay at the cash desk.*

Numbers, Weights and Measures→7, Clothing→19

1 You want to change some money. What sign do you look for?

2 You enter a shop. What does the shop assistant ask you?

3 You are just looking. What do you tell the shop assistant?

4 You want to know whether she has got any T-shirts. What do you say?

5 Read out the prices of these two T-shirts.

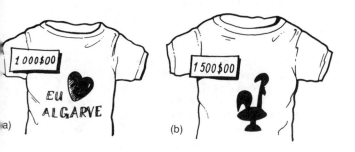

(a)   (b)

6 You choose a T-shirt and want to know how much it costs. What do you say?

7 The shop assistant wants to know whether you would like anything else. What does she ask?

8 You want to answer *No, thank you*. What do you say?

9 The assistant tells you to pay at the cash desk. What does she say?

Here is a receipt from a souvenir shop for a filigree brooch and an ornamental tile.

```
054-01  Filigrana   6 010 $ 00
054-01  Azulejo        89 $ 50

        Total       6 099 $ 50

É favor conservar o recibo.
```

10 How much did the filigree item cost?

11 How much did the tile cost?

12 How much did the customer pay altogether?

- The Portuguese currency unit is the **escudo**. It is divided
  into 100 **centavos**. The symbol for the escudo is **$**. It is
  placed between the escudo and centavo units: 50$50 (50
  escudos and 50 centavos). One thousand escudos is
  known as **conto**: 2 000$00 (dois mil escudos or dois
  contos).

- **Banks** are usually open from 8.30 to 11.45 am and 1 to
  2.45 pm, Monday to Friday. In Lisbon, some central
  branches are also open between 6 and 11 pm. In the
  Algarve, the bank at Vilamoura is open daily from 9 am
  to 9 pm.

- **Shops** are open in general from 9 am to 1 pm and 3 pm to
  7 pm, from Monday to Friday. On Saturdays they are
  open between 9 am and 1 pm. Shopping centres are open
  from 10 am to 11 pm including Saturdays.

- Here are the names of some shops:
  - a **alimentação** ⎫ *grocer's*
  - a **mercearia** ⎬
  - a **padaria**   *baker's*
  - a **leitaria**   *dairy*
  - a **peixaria**   *fishmonger's*
  - o **talho**   *butcher's*
  - o **lugar de hortaliça**   *greengrocer's*
  - a **farmácia**   *chemist's*
  - o **sapateiro**   *cobbler's*
  - a **loja de lembranças** ⎫ *souvenir shop*
  - a **loja de artesanato** ⎬
  - a **livraria**   *bookshop*
  - a **loja de ferragens**   *hardware*
  - o **quiosque de jornais**   *news-stand*

a. Meals **b.** Tableware **c.** Breakfast **d.** Snacks

a	**refeição**	*meal*
o	**pequeno almoço**	*breakfast*
o	**almoço**	*lunch*
o	**lanche**	*afternoon snack*
o	**jantar**	*dinner, supper*
a	**ceia**	*late evening snack*
	comer	*eat*
	beber	*drink*
a	**sala de jantar**	*dining-room*
a	**chávena**	*cup*
o	**copo**	*glass*
a	**garrafa**	*bottle*
o	**jarro**	*jug*
o	**prato**	*plate, dish*
a	**taça**	*dessert dish*
a	**colher**	*spoon*
o	**garfo**	*fork*
a	**faca**	*knife*
o	**guardanapo**	*napkin*
a	**toalha**	*table-cloth*

Uma chávena de café.	*A cup of coffee.*
Uma garrafa de vinho.	*A bottle of wine.*
Um copo d'água.	*A glass of water.*

c.

o	**pão**	bread
o	**pão de forma**	loaf
o	**pão caseiro**	farmhouse loaf
o	**pãozinho**, os **pãezinhos**	roll, rolls
o	**cacete**	stick (loaf)
a	**torrada**	slice of toast
a	**manteiga**	butter
a	**geléia**	jam
a	**geléia de laranja**	marmalade
o	**café**	coffee
o	**chá**	tea
o	**chocolate**	hot chocolate
o	**sumo de fruta**	fruit juice

Café ou chá?	*Coffee or tea?*
Um café com leite.	*A white coffee.*
Chá simples ou com limão?	*Tea with or without lemon? (Plain tea or tea with lemon?)*
Um chá com leite.	*A cup of tea (served with milk)*
Um chá de limão.	*A cup of lemon tea (infusion of lemon peel)*
Com açúcar ou sem açúcar.	*With sugar or without sugar.*
Torrada com manteiga.	*Buttered toast.*

d.

a	**sanduíche**	sandwich
o	**fiambre**	ham
o	**queijo**	cheese
a	**omeleta**	omelette
as	**batatas fritas**	chips/crisps
o	**bolo**	cake

Tem sanduíches?	*Do you have sandwiches?*
Uma sanduíche de fiambre.	*A ham sandwich.*
Um cachorro.	*A hot dog.*
Uma omeleta de camarão.	*A prawn omelette.*

Paying→9, Restaurants→11, Drinking→14

1 What are the three meals of the day called in Portuguese?

2 What are the following called in Portuguese?

(a)   *(b)*   *(c)*   *(d)*   *(e)*   *(f)*

3 What do you call these in Portuguese?

(a)   *(b)*

4 You want your tea served with milk. What do you ask for?

5 How do you ask for a drink of fruit juice?

6   You would like a glass of wine. What do you say?

7   How do you ask for a cheese sandwich?

8   Ask for a ham omelette.

– **Meals:** In Portugal, breakfast is a light meal consisting of black or white coffee, bread, butter and jam. Most people have a cooked meal for lunch (usually around 1 pm). A light afternoon snack is often eaten around 5 pm. Dinner is also a cooked meal and is eaten after 8 pm. If you go out in the evening, you may need a late evening snack.

– Some popular **snacks**:

um rissol de camarão	a prawn pasty
um pastel de bacalhau	a dried cod fish-cake
um croquete	a minced-beef croquette
uma empada	a small meat pie
carnes frias	cooked meats

Also: small open pastry pies with an endless variety of sweet fillings, amongst them:

um pastel de nata (with a flavoured egg and cream custard)

uma queijada (with a cheese mixture)

1 Restaurants

o	**restaurante**	*restaurant*
o	**café**	*café, bar*
o	**bar**	*bar*
a	**cervejaria**	*beer-house*
a	**pastelaria,** a **confeitaria**	*cake and snack-shop*
o	**salão de chá**	*tea and cake-shop*
a	**mesa**	*table*
a	**cadeira**	*chair*
a	**esplanada**	*terrace, outdoor café/cake-shop*

É para comer.	*I/We would like to eat.*
Quantas pessoas?	*How many people?*
Tem uma mesa para três?	*Do you have a table for three?*
Há uma mesa vaga.	*There's a free table.*

b.

	a	**ementa, a lista**	*menu*
		pedir	*order*
	o	**prato do dia**	*dish of the day*
		beber um aperitivo	*have a pre-dinner drink*
	os	**aperitivos, os acepipes**	*appetizers*
	a	**entrada, o hors d'oeuvre**	*starter, hors d'oeuvre*
	o	**prato**	*course, dish*
	a	**sobremesa**	*dessert*
	o	**queijo**	*cheese*
	o	**café**	*coffee*
	a	**carta dos vinhos**	*wine-list*

A ementa, f.f..	*Could I/we have the menu, please?*
Traga-me este prato, f.f..	*Bring me this dish, please.*
Que deseja beber?	*What would you like to drink?*
Que sobremesa deseja?	*What would you like for dessert?*
Esta sobremesa.	*This dessert.*
Já pedi.	*I'm being served.*

c.

o	**açúcar**	*sugar*
o	**sal**/a **pimenta**	*salt/pepper*
o	**azeite**/o **vinagre**	*oil (olive oil)/vinegar*

d.

a	**conta**	*bill*
	serviço (não) incluído	*service (not) included*
a	**gorjeta**	*tip*

Faz favor!	*Waiter!/Waitress!*
A conta, f.f..	*Could I/We have the bill, please?*
O troco é para si.	*Keep the change.*

Toilets→6, Paying→9, Meals→10, Drinking→14

11 Restaurants

1 Where do you go
   (a) if you want lunch?
   (b) if you want mainly a drink?
   (c) if you want mainly cakes?

2 What are these called in Portuguese?

(a)

(b)

3 You are in a restaurant. Ask the waiter whether he has a table for 2?

4 Ask for the menu and the wine list.

5 You want to order the 'dish of the day' for one person. What do you say?

6 The waiter asks what you would like to drink. What does he say?

7 Attract the waiter's attention and ask him to bring you the oil and vinegar.

8 What are the following called in Portuguese?

(b)   *(c)*

(a)

9 How do you ask for your bill?

10 The waiter wants to give you back the change, but you want him to keep it as a tip. What do you say?

– There are four categories of **restaurants**, from luxury (**de luxo**) to 3rd class (**3ª classe**), but you will find out that Portuguese people enjoy their food and you will not have to go to an expensive restaurant to eat well. The 'dish of the day' (**o prato do dia**) is usually the best choice. For dinner you may wish to go to a fado club (**a casa de fado**). Here you can have a meal while you listen to typically Portuguese songs.

– **The bill** usually includes the service charge, but it is customary to leave an additional tip of approximately 10% for the waiter.

– Naturally, a café specializes in coffee, a tea-shop in tea and a beer house in beer, but in these shops you can also drink something else and eat a snack. A **pastelaria** (or **confeitaria**) is mainly a cake-shop, but most have a delicatessen counter, and you can also have something to drink, alcoholic or not, including coffee and tea. For a light meal there are snack-bars (**o snack-bar**).

– **Take-away:** From most pastelarias you can buy, at the counter, snacks and cakes to take away (**para embrulhar**). You can also buy snacks from a delicatessen shop (**a charcutaria**), where you will find a wide variety of cooked meats and smoked sausages. Other sources of snacks are mini-markets, supermarkets and hypermarkets (**o mini-mercado, o supermercado, o hipermercado**).

– **Portuguese cheese:** Most are a blend of goat's milk with either sheep's or cow's milk. Your menu is likely to include **queijo da Serra da Estrela**, a creamy cured cheese, and **queijo flamengo**, which is a bit like Gouda. **Queijo fresco** is a bland white cheese slightly resembling cottage cheese; it is often served as an appetizer.

. Starters b. Meat c. Poultry, Eggs d. Fish

.	a **sopa**	*soup*
	a **canja**	*chicken broth*
	o **caldo verde**	*shredded kale soup*
	a **açorda**	*bread soup*
	o **consomé**	*clear soup, consommé*
	o **gaspacho**	*cold vegetable soup*

A sopa de legumes.	*Vegetable soup.*
A sopa de tomate.	*Tomato soup.*
A açorda com ovo escalfado.	*Bread soup with poached egg.*
Os acepipes variados.	*A variety of cold meats, tinned sardines, pickles, etc.*

.	a **carne**	*meat*
	Vaca	*Beef*
	Vitela	*Veal*

	Porco	*Pork*
	Caça	*Game*
a	**costeleta**	*chop*
o	**bife**	*(beef) steak*
a	**febra**	*lean pork steak*
o	**entrecosto**	*rib steak*
a	**pasta (de fígado)**	*(liver) paté*
o	**molho**	*sauce, gravy*

Como deseja o bife?	*How would you like your steak?*
Mal passado? Médio? Bem passado?	*Rare? Medium? Well done?*
Guisado de borrego.	*Lamb stew.*
Leitão assado.	*Roast sucking pig.*
Espetada mista.	*Mixed kebab.*
Cozido à portuguesa.	*Boiled beef, smoked sausage and vegetables.*
Feijoada.	*Meat and dried beans stew.*

c.

	Aves	*Poultry*
o	**frango**	*chicken*
o	**pato**	*duck*
o	**ovo**	*egg*

Frango no churrasco.	*Barbecued chicken (on the spit).*
Um ovo bem cozido.	*A hard-boiled egg.*
Um ovo mal cozido.	*A soft boiled egg.*
Ovos estrelados.	*Fried eggs.*
Uma omeleta de presunto.	*A bacon omelette.*

d.

	Peixe	*Fish*
o	**linguado**	*sole*
o	**bacalhau**	*cod(dried)*
	Marisco	*Shellfish*
os	**camarões**	*prawns*

Sardinhas assadas na brasa.	*Sardines grilled on the embers.*
Amêijoas ao natural.	*Steamed clams.*
Caldeirada.	*Fish stew.*

sk for the following in Portuguese.

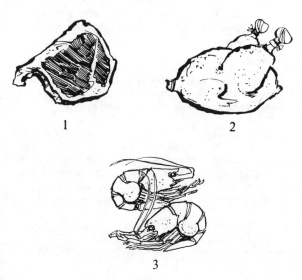

1

2

3

hat do you say to the waiter:

4   if you want vegetable soup?

    if you want tomato soup with poached egg?

5   if you want your steak well done?

7   if you want your steak rare?

3   if you want liver paté?

)   if you want a fried egg?

)   if you want fish stew for three?

- Popular starters are **queijo fresco** (bland soft white cheese), **melão com presunto** (a slice of melon and bacon) and **amêijoas ao natural** (steamed clams), amongst others.

- **Shellfish** is served on its own or as one of the ingredients in a variety of dishes. In **cataplana**, mussels or clams are cooked with ham, sausage and vegetables. **Carne de porco à alentejana** combines pork with clams.

- **Sardinhas assadas** are fresh sardines grilled on a charcoal fire and usually eaten with a tomato and green pepper salad. Different kinds of fish are combined in the fish stew **caldeirada**. **Bacalhau**—dried salted cod—is said to be the national dish of Portugal and be cooked in at least 365 different ways, one for each day of the year.

- **Refogado** (fried onion and tomato purée) is the basis for a large number of fish and meat dishes.

a. Vegetables **b.** Fruit **c.** Desserts, Sweets

a.		**Legumes**	*Vegetables*
	as	**batatas**	*potatoes*
	as	**batatas fritas**	*chips*
	os	**tomates**	*tomatoes*
	o	**pepino**	*cucumber*
	as	**cenouras**	*carrots*
	as	**ervilhas**	*green peas*
	os	**feijões verdes**	*runner-beans*
	a	**couve**	*cabbage*

a	**cebola**	*onion*
o	**alho**	*garlic*
os	**cogumelos**	*mushrooms*
as	**alcachofras**	*artichokes*
o	**arroz**	*rice*

Salada de tomate e alface, f.f..	*Tomato and lettuce salad, please.*
Tomates recheados.	*Stuffed tomatoes.*
Arroz de marisco.	*Rice with shellfish.*

b.

	Fruta	*Fruit*
a	**maçã**	*apple*
a	**pera**	*pear*
a	**laranja**	*orange*
o	**limão**	*lemon*
a	**banana**	*banana*
o	**figo**	*fig*
a	**ameixa**	*plum*
as	**cerejas**	*cherries*
os	**morangos**	*strawberries*
o	**melão**	*melon*
a	**melancia**	*water-melon*
as	**uvas**	*grapes*

Morangos com açúcar.	*Strawberries with sugar.*
Pêssegos com porto.	*Peaches with Port.*
Ananás com madeira.	*Pineapple with Madeira.*
Salada de fruta.	*Fruit salad.*

c.

	Doces	*Sweets*
o	**pudim**	*pudding*
a	**tarte**	*tart*
a	**nata**	*cream*
	Gelados	*Ice cream/ice lollies*
o	**sorvete**	*sorbet, ice cream*
a	**baunilha**	*vanilla*

Um pudim flan.	*A caramel custard.*
Um mousse de chocolate.	*A chocolate mousse.*
Gosto de sorvete de morango.	*I like strawberry ice cream.*

What are the following in Portuguese? Say you like them.
Example: **Os feijões verdes. Gosto de feijões verdes.**

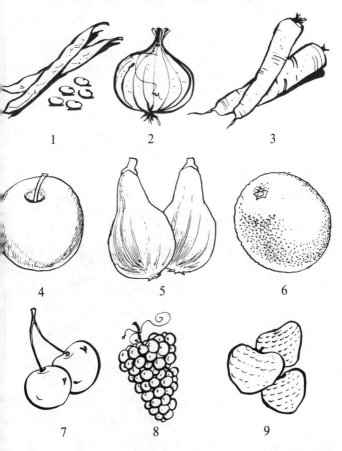

1

2

3

4

5

6

7

8

9

0 Ask for a tomato and lettuce salad.

1 Ask for strawberries with cream.

2 You want a vanilla and chocolate ice cream. What do
   you say?

– In Portugal, a piece of fruit or a fruit salad is often eaten as a dessert. Instead, or in addition to this, you can also have a pudding.

– Sugar, eggs and almonds provide the basic ingredients for most Portuguese sweets and puddings.

– Some popular desserts and sweets:
- **maçã assada** – sugary baked apple;
- **marmelada** – quince fruit paste (from **o marmelo**, quince);
- **pudim flan** (also spelt **flã**) – caramel custard;
- **leite de creme** – custard cream, often served with **farófias**, beaten egg whites cooked in milk;
- **arroz doce** – rich sweet rice decorated with powdered cinnamon;
- **pudim molotov** – egg white mousse in caramel sauce;
- **ovos moles** (soft eggs), **fios d'ovos** (golden hair), and **trouxas** (bundles), are all variations of a mixture of sugar and eggs;
- **dom rodrigos** and **morgados** are two of the best-known sweets made out of an almond and sugar mixture.

a. Non-alcoholic Beverages
b. Alcoholic Beverages   **c.** Smoking

a.	as **bebidas**	*drinks*
	os **refrigerantes,** ⎫	
	os **refrescos** ⎭	*refreshments*
	a **laranjada**	*orangeade*
	a **limonada**	*lemonade*
	a **cola**	*cola*
	o **sumo**	*juice*
	o **sumo de laranja**	*orange juice*
	a **água**	*water*
	a **água mineral**	*mineral water*
	o **leite**	*milk*
	o **batido**	*milkshake*
	o **chá**	*plain tea*

o **café, a bica**   *black coffee*
o **galão**   *white coffee (served in a tall glass)*

Tenho sede.	*I'm thirsty.*
Um sumo de ananás, f.f..	*A pineapple juice, please.*
Um copo d'água mineral.	*A glass of mineral water.*
Uma bica com açúcar.	*A black coffee with sugar.*
Dois galões sem açúcar.	*Two glasses of white coffee without sugar.*

b.
a **cerveja**   *beer*
o **vinho**   *wine*
o **champanhe**   *champagne*
a **cidra**   *cider*
o **licor**   *liqueur*
o **conhaque**   *cognac*
a **garrafa**   *bottle*
o **abre-garrafas**   *bottle-opener*
o **saca-rolhas**   *corkscrew*

O vinho branco/rosado/tinto.	*White wine/rosé/red wine.*
Uma garrafa de vinho.	*A bottle of wine.*
Uma meia garrafa de vinho.	*A half-bottle of wine.*
Uma imperial e um prato de tremoços.	*A glass of lager and a dish of tremoços.*
Saúde!	*Cheers!*

c.
o **cigarro**   *cigarette*
o **charuto**   *cigar*
o **isqueiro**   *lighter*
o **fósforo**   *match*
o **cinzeiro**   *ashtray*
a **tabacaria**   *tobacconist*

Deseja um cigarro?	*Would you like a cigarette?*
Um maço de cigarros.	*A packet of cigarettes.*
Com ou sem filtro?	*With or without filter?*
Uma caixa de fósforos.	*A box of matches.*
Proibido fumar/Não fumar.	*No smoking.*

Meals→10

sk for

1 An apple juice.

2 An orangeade.

3 Two colas.

4 A bottle of mineral water.

5 Two black coffees.

6 A tea with milk and sugar.

7 A glass of white wine.

8 A bottle of red wine.

9 How do you ask for these?

What are these called in Portuguese?

10

11

12

13

14 What do you say if you want to offer someone a cigarette?

- A black coffee, **um café**, is also known as **uma bica**, mainly in Lisbon and the Algarve. It is served in a small cup or glass. **Um carioca** is a black coffee diluted in hot water and **um garoto** is a white coffee. White coffee served in a larger cup is **uma meia** and served in a tall glass is **um galão**.

- **Chá com limão** is China tea served with lemon juice or a slice of lemon. **Chá de limão** is an infusion of lemon peel.

- **Wine** is drunk at mealtimes by adults whilst children drink fruit juice, just water or a little wine diluted in water. Portugal is famous for its variety of good wines. There is **vinho verde**, a crisp refreshing wine from Minho; the dry velvety Dão red wine; the Bairrada and Douro fruity red wines; the Borba, Redondo, Reguengos and Vidigueira red wines from the Alentejo; rosés from different areas; fortified wines Porto and Madeira; and also the various Portuguese brandies including **aguardente, bagaceira, medronho** and **moscatel**.

- It is quite safe to drink tap water anywhere unless a notice says otherwise (**água não potável**). Bottled mineral water is available throughout the country.

- Cigarettes and tobacco can be bought mainly at tobacco shops (**a tabacaria**) or the tobacco counter you will find in some cafés. A wide range of Portuguese and imported brands is available.
  Smoking is not allowed in theatres, cinemas, indoor sports arenas and urban transport.

---

a. Tourism **b.** Places of Interest
c. Entertainment **d.** Admission

a.

o	**turista**	*tourist*
o	**centro de turismo**	*tourist information office*
o	**folheto**	*brochure*
a	**agência de viagens**	*travel agency*

Onde é o turismo?	*Where is the tourist office?*
Tem folhetos de informação?	*Do you have any brochures?*

b.

as	**atracções**	*sights*
o	**museu**	*museum*
o	**castelo**	*castle*
o	**palácio**	*palace*
a	**igreja**	*church*

| a | **sé (catedral)** | *cathedral* |
| a | **romaria** | *country pilgrimage* |

A Torre de Belém.	*The Tower of Belém.*
Desejo ver o Padrão aos Descobrimentos.	*I'd like to see the Monument to the Discoveries.*
Visitar o Mosteiro dos Jerónimos.	*Visit the Heronymites Monastery.*

c.

o	**teatro**	*theatre*
o	**cinema**	*cinema*
a	**buate**	*night-club*
a	**casa de fado**	*fado club*
o	**salão de concertos**	*concert-hall*
a	**festa**	*festival*
o	**estádio**	*stadium*

Vamos para a casa de fado.	*We are going to the fado club.*
Vamos para o estádio.	*We are going to the stadium.*
A que horas começa o espectáculo?	*At what time does the performance start?*
A que horas acaba?	*At what time does it end?*

d.

as	**horas de abertura**	*opening hours*
	aberto	*open*
	fechado	*closed*
a	**entrada**	*entrance*
a	**saída**	*exit*
	Empurrar/Empurre	*Push*
	Puxar/Puxe	*Pull*
a	**bilheteira**	*ticket window*
o	**bilhete**	*ticket*
o	**guia, a guia**	*male guide, female guide*
	visitar	*visit, tour*

O seu bilhete, f.f..	*Your ticket, please.*
Uma volta guiada.	*A conducted tour.*

5 Sightseeing and Entertainment

Do you know these tourist attractions in the Great Lisbon area?

1

2

3

4 You are looking for the tourist office. Ask where it is.

5 Say that you would like to visit the palace.

6   Say that you would like to see the festival.

7   You are going to a concert and would like to know at
    what time the performance starts. What do you say?

You're visiting a museum. Which sign do you look for

8   to find out the opening times?

9   when you want to buy admission tickets?

10   Which sign indicates the entrance?

11   Which sign indicates the exit?

12   The museum, the shop or the garage is closed. What
     does the sign say?

– **Tourist Information Offices** are open on weekdays from
9 am to 7 pm. Some are closed on Sundays and public
holidays. Staff is multilingual and will provide you with
brochures and information including news of local
events and festivals. This information can also be
obtained from:

> Portuguese National Tourist Office
> 1/5 New Bond Street
> London W1Y ONP
> Tel: (021) 493 3873

– **National public holidays** are as follows:
1 January; Shrove Tuesday and Good Friday (movable
dates); 25 April; 1 May; Corpus Christi (movable date);
10 June; 15 August; 5 October; 1 November; 1, 8 and
25 December.

a. Excursions **b.** Scenery **c.** Sports
d. Photography

a.

a	**excursão**	*excursion, outing*
a	**volta**	*tour*
o	**miradouro**	*vantage point, view point*

> Vamos fazer uma excursão. *We're going on an outing.*
> A volta Lisboa-Estoril-Sintra. *A tour of Lisbon, Estoril and Sintra.*

b.

o	**mar**	*sea*
o	**oceano**	*ocean*
o	**Atlântico**	*Atlantic (ocean)*
a	**costa,** o **litoral**	*coast*
a	**gruta**	*cave*

a	**rocha**	*rock*
o	**rio**	*river*
o	**lago**	*lake*
a	**serra**	*mountain-range*
a	**mata**	*wood*
o	**parque**	*park*
o	**jardim**	*park, gardens*

Vejo o rio.	*I (can) see the river.*
Coimbra e o Rio Mondego.	*The town of Coimbra and the River Mondego.*
A Serra da Estrela.	*The Star Mountains.*
A costa do Algarve.	*The Algarve coast.*

c.

a	**praia**	*beach*
a	**piscina**	*swimming-pool*
o	**vestiário**	*changing-room*
o	**toldo**	*sun-shade*
a	**barraca**	*beach-hut*
	nadar	*swim*
	bronzear	*tan*
o	**barco à vela**	*sailing-boat*
a	**pesca**	*fishing*
	esquiar	*to ski*

A piscina aquecida.	*Heated pool.*
Desejo fazer esqui aquático.	*I'd like to go water skiing.*
Desejo alugar . . .	*I'd like to hire . . .*
Vamos dar um passeio.	*We're going for a walk.*

d.

a	**máquina fotográfica**	*camera*
o	**rolo (de películas)**	*film*
o	**flash**	*flash*
a	**pilha**	*battery*
a	**fotografia, a foto**	*photo*

Tem filmes a cores?	*Do you have any colour films?*
Um rolo, f.f..	*A film, please.*
O flash não funciona.	*The flash isn't working.*

What can you see in these pictures? Answer in Portuguese, beginning **Vejo** . . . (*I can see* . . .)

The Star Mountains

The town of Coimbra and River Mondego

A beach in the Algarve

What sign do you look for

4 when you want to go to the swimming-pool?

5   when you want the changing-room?

6   Say that you would like to hire a sailing-boat.

What are these called in Portuguese?

rope — canvas — Wooden post

7

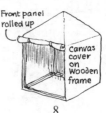

Front panel rolled up

Canvas cover on Wooden frame

8

You would like to buy the following items. How do you ask for them?

9

10

11

- There is a place of tourist interest almost anywhere in Portugal depending on your preferences: over 500 miles of beaches; vineyards on hill slopes, mountain ridges covered with snow, ancient castles and ruins, or cosmopolitan holiday resorts. The best known tourist areas from north to south along the coast are Costa Verde; Costa de Prata, Lisbon-Estoril-Sintra; and the Algarve. Inland, you have the plains of Alentejo and the mountains of the Beiras and Trás-os-Montes. On the Atlantic, the islands of Madeira and Açores (the Azores).

- Popular leisure activities for holidaymakers in Portugal are tennis, golf, fishing, shooting, sailing, horse-riding, waterskiing, windsurfing and scuba-diving. In Serra da Estrela (Beira) there is a winter sports centre.

a. The Weather **b.** Good Weather
c. Bad Weather **d.** Cold Weather

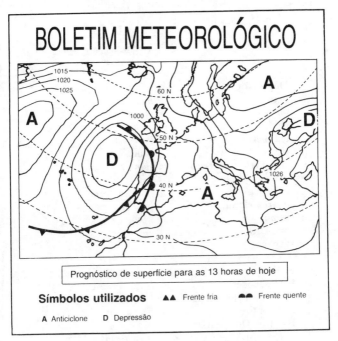

BOLETIM METEOROLÓGICO

Prognóstico de superfície para as 13 horas de hoje

Símbolos utilizados   ▲▲ Frente fria   ●● Frente quente

A Anticiclone   D Depressão

a.			
o	**boletim meteorológico**		*weather report*
o	**tempo**		*weather*
a	**maré**		*tide*

Que tempo vai fazer?	*What's the weather going to be like?*
Que tempo faz?	*What's the weather like?*

b.		
o	**bom tempo**	*good weather*
o	**sol**	*sun*
a	**temperatura**	*temperature*
	quente	*warm, hot*
o	**calor**	*heat*
	Anticiclone (A)	*high-pressure area*

Faz bom tempo.	*The weather is good.*
Faz calor./Está quente.	*It's warm, hot.*
Faz sol.	*The sun is shining.*
Estão 25 graus à sombra.	*It's 25 degrees (=77°F) in the shade.*
A água está boa.	*The water is warm. (= The water is good.)*

c.

	Depressão (D)	*low-pressure area*
o	**mau tempo**	*bad weather*
a	**nuvem**	*cloud*
	nublado	*cloudy*
	encoberto	*overcast*
a	**chuva**	*rain*
a	**chuvada**/o **aguaceiro**	*shower*
o	**granizo**	*hail*
a	**trovoada**	*thunderstorm*
o	**guarda-chuva**	*umbrella*
o	**vento**	*wind*
o	**nevoeiro**	*fog*
a	**neblina**	*mist*

Faz mau tempo.	*The weather is bad.*
Está encoberto.	*It is overcast.*
Faz chuva./Está a chover.	*It's raining.*
Faz vento.	*It is windy.*
Faz trovoada./Está a trovejar.	*It is stormy.*

d.

	frio	*cold*
o	**gelo**	*ice*
a	**geada**	*frost*
a	**neve**	*snow*

Faz frio./Está frio.	*It's cold.*
Faz neve./Está a nevar.	*It's snowing.*

Look at this weather map from the Portuguese newspaper
O País:

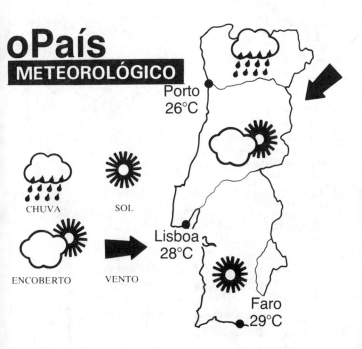

1   What is the weather like
    (*a*) in the North?
    (*b*) in the Centre?
    (*c*) in the South?

2   What is the temperature
    (*a*) in Lisbon? (*b*) in Oporto? (*c*) in Faro?

What's the weather like?

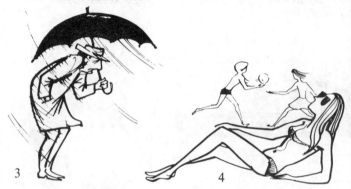

3

4

Look at the following information on high tide (**preia-
-mar**) and low tide (**baixa-mar**).

5   At what time is high tide?

6   At what time is low tide?

PREIA-MAR
01.52 e 14.17

BAIXA-MAR
07.45 e 19.57

marés

– In Portugal temperatures are given in **Centigrade**
(Celsius). To convert them into Fahrenheit, multiply by
1.8 (or 9/5) and add 32.

Celsius	−5	0	5	10	15	20	25	30	35
Fahrenheit	23	32	41	50	59	68	77	86	95

a. Post Office   **b.** Letters and Postcards
c. Telephone

a.	o	**correio**	*post-office/post*
	o	**postigo,** o **guichê**	*service window*
	o	**marco do correio**	*letter-box*

| Faz favor, onde é o correio? | *Excuse me please, where is the post-office?* |

b.

a	**carta**	*letter*
o	**postal,** os **postais**	*postcard, postcards*
o	**endereço**	*address*
o	**código postal**	*postcode*
o	**selo**	*stamp*
o	**telegrama**	*telegram*
o	**impresso**	*form*
o	**expedidor**	*sender*
a	**caneta**	*pen*
	por avião/via aérea	*air mail*

| Quanto é um selo para . . .? | *How much is a stamp for . . .?* |
| Um selo para postal para Inglaterra, f.f.. | *A stamp for a postcard to England, please.* |

c.

o	**telefone**	*telephone*
o	**número do telefone**	*telephone number*
o	**indicativo**	*area code*
a	**lista telefónica**	*telephone-book*
a	**cabina telefónica**	*telephone-box*
o	**auscultador**	*receiver*
a	**telefonista**	*lady operator*
a	**chamada a ser paga pelo destinatário**	*reverse-charge call*

Qual é o número do seu telefone?	*What's your telephone number?*
Está lá?	*Hello!*
É de 33-50-74?	*Is that 33-50-74?*
Não desligue, f.f..	*Hold the line, please.*

Numbers→7, Money→9

hat are these called in Portuguese?

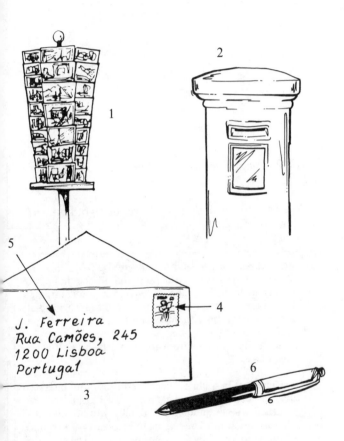

You want to buy stamps for two postcards to England. What do you ask for?

You would like someone's telephone number. What do you ask him/her?

9   What is this called in Portuguese?

10   You telephone someone. What will you hear for *Hello!*

11   You want to check that you have the right number. What do you say?

– **Post-offices** are open from 9 am until 7 pm. They are closed on Saturdays, Sundays and public holidays, though major branch offices open on Saturday morning. In Lisbon there is a 24-hour service at the airport and at the Praça dos Restauradores office.

– You can buy **stamps** from tobacconists' as well as at post-offices.

– **Telephones:** In public telephone-boxes you insert a number of the required coins; unused coins will be returned. A continuous sound tells you to dial the number you want. The ringing tone consists of 1 second of sound followed by 5 seconds of silence. The engaged tone is a short intermittent sound.

19 Clothing and Toiletries

a. Clothing **b.** Socks and Shoes **c.** Colours
d. Toiletries **e.** At the Hairdresser's

Roupa para Homem	*Roupa para Senhora*

a.

a	**roupa**	*clothes*
a	**camisola**	*pullover, sweater*
o	**vestido**	*dress*
a	**blusa**	*blouse*
a	**saia**	*skirt*
a	**camisa**	*shirt*
o	**casaco**	*jacket, coat*
as	**calças**	*trousers*
o	**cinto**	*belt*
o	**chapéu**	*hat*
o	**lenço**	*scarf*
as	**luvas**	*gloves*
o	**impermeável**	*raincoat*
o	**fato de banho**	*swimming costume*
o	**calção de banho**	*swimming trunks*
o	**biquini**	*bikini*
as	**cabinas de prova**	*changing-rooms*

Roupa para Homem.	*Men's wear.*
Roupa para Senhora.	*Women's wear.*
Desejo uma blusa.	*I'd like a blouse.*
Um par de calças.	*A pair of trousers.*
Posso provar?	*May I try it on?*
É grande/pequeno.	*It's too big/small.*
É curto/comprido.	*It's too short/long.*
Não gosto.	*I don't like it.*
Fico com este(*m.*)/esta(*f*)	*I will take this one.*

b.

os	**sapatos**	*shoes*
as	**sandálias**	*sandals*
as	**peúgas**/as **meias**	*socks*
as	**meias**	*stockings*
os	**colans**	*tights*

Desejo um par de sapatos.	*I'd like a pair of shoes.*
Que tamanho?	*What size?*

c.

a	**cor**	*colour*
	branco, preto	*white, black*
	cinzento	*grey*
	vermelho, verde	*red, green*
	azul, amarelo	*blue, yellow*
	castanho	*brown*

d.

o	**sabonete**	*toilet soap*
o	**shampô**	*shampoo*
a	**toalha**	*towel*
a	**pasta dentífrica**	*toothpaste*
a	**escova para dentes**	*toothbrush*
a	**máquina de barbear**	*electric razor*
a	**água de colónia**	*Cologne*
o	**perfume**	*perfume*
o	**penso higiénico**	*sanitary towel*
a	**fralda**	*nappy*
o	**lenço**	*handkerchief*
o	**bronzeador**	*suntan oil*
os	**óculos**	*glasses*

Tem lenços de papel?	*Do you have paper tissues?*
Os óculos de sol.	*Sunglasses.*

e.

o	**cabeleireiro**	*hairdresser*
o	**barbeiro**	*barber*
a	**escova**	*brush*
o	**pente**	*comb*

Para cortar, f.f..	*A haircut, please.*
Para lavar e fazer mise.	*A shampoo and set.*
Com secador de mão.	*Blow-dry.*
Corte e barba, f.f..	*A haircut and a shave, please.*

Money, shopping→9

Say that you would like to buy these:

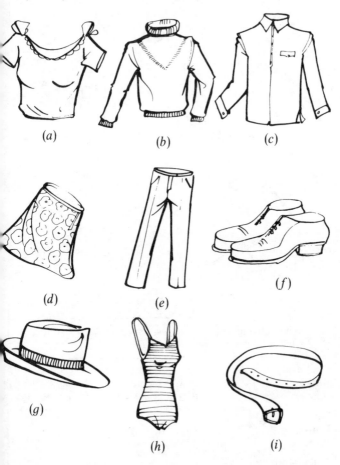

(a)

(b)

(c)

(d)

(e)

(f)

(g)

(h)

(i)

Ask permission to try on what you have chosen.

Say that it's too small.

You have found a pair of shoes that fit you. Say that you will have *this one*.

Ask the chemist whether he has these:

5

6

7

8

9

– When buying **clothes** or **shoes**, remember that Portuguese sizes are different from British ones.

Shoe sizes

British	1	2	3	4	5	6	7	8	9	10	11	12
Port.	33	34–35	36	37	38	39–40	41	42	43	44	45	46

Dress sizes

British	10	12	14	16	18	20
Port.	38	40	42	44	46	48

Collar sizes

British	13	$13\frac{1}{2}$	14	$14\frac{1}{2}$	15	$15\frac{1}{2}$	16	$16\frac{1}{2}$	17
Port.	33	34	35–36	37	38	39	41	42	43

Suits, coats

British	36	38	40	42	44	46
Port.	46	48	50	52	54	56

a. Car breakdown, Accidents **b.** Theft
c. Police **d.** Illness **e.** Chemist **f.** Doctor
g. Help!

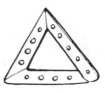

a	**avaria,** a **pane**	*breakdown*
o	**desastre,** o **acidente**	*accident*
o	**choque**	*collision, crash*
a	**garagem**	*garage*
o	**seguro**	*insurance*

Onde há uma garagem?	*Where is there a garage?*
Tenho o carro avariado.	*My car has broken down.*
Houve um desastre.	*There has been an accident.*
Preciso de um rebocador.	*I want/need a towing-truck.*
A sua apólice de seguro?	*Your insurance papers?*
A culpa não é minha.	*It's not my fault.*

	perder	*lose*
	roubar	*steal*
o	**ladrão**	*thief*
o	**porta-moedas**	*purse*
	Perdidos e Achados	*Lost property*

Perdi as chaves.	*I've lost my keys.*
Roubaram-me a carteira/ o carro.	*My wallet/car has been stolen.*
Não sei.	*I don't know.*

a	**polícia**	*police*
a	**infracção**	*offence*
o	**advogado**	*lawyer*

Chame a polícia!	*Call the police!*
O polícia.	*Policeman.*
Desejo um intérprete.	*I would like an interpreter.*

d.

	doente	*ill*
a	**queimadura de sol**	*sunburn*
a	**dor de cabeça**	*headache*
a	**constipação**	*cold*
o	**ataque de coração**	*heart attack*

Estou doente.	*I'm ill.*
Tenho uma constipação.	*I have a cold.*
Tenho uma dor de estômago.	*I have a stomach-ache.*
Tenho uma dor de dentes.	*I have a toothache.*
Tenho febre.	*I have a fever.*
Estou ferido (m.)/ferida(f.)	*I am injured.*

e.

a	**farmácia**	*chemist's, pharmacy*
o	**medicamento, o remédio**	*medicine*
a	**pomada**	*ointment*
o	**comprimido**	*tablet*
a	**drageia**	*dragée, pill*
o	**penso adesivo**	*sticking-plaster*
a	**ligadura**	*bandage*

Farmácia de serviço.	*Chemist on emergency duty.*
Ligaduras, f.f..	*Some bandages, please.*

f.

o	**médico**	*doctor*
o	**dentista**	*dentist*
o	**posto de socorros**	*first aid*
o	**hospital**	*hospital*
a	**ambulância**	*ambulance*

Chame um médico, depressa!	*Get a doctor, quick!*
Chame uma ambulância.	*Call an ambulance.*
Não é grave.	*It's not serious.*

g.

Perigo	*Danger*
Atenção, Cuidado	*Caution*
ajudar	*help*

Pode ajudar-me?	*Can you help me?*
Socorro!	*Help!*
Saída de Emergência.	*Emergency Exit.*

You are telephoning a garage. Tell the mechanic that your car has broken down.

You are involved in an accident. How do you ask someone to call the police?

How do you say that there has been an accident?

You were not to blame for the accident. What do you tell the police?

Tell the police that you have lost your passport.

Say that your purse has been stolen.

You have witnessed an accident. How do you ask someone to call an ambulance?

Tell the dentist you have a toothache.

You are not feeling well and go to the doctor's. Tell him you have:
(a) a headache; (b) sunburn; (c) a fever.

The doctor does not think it is serious. What does he say?

Ask the chemist for:
(a) some ointment; (b) some sticking plasters; (c) some medicine.

(a) You feel suddenly ill when swimming in the sea and you are in risk of drowning. How do you shout for help?
(b) You are locked inside a building. How do you shout for help through the window?

– **Emergencies** – The Portuguese equivalent of 999 is 115.

– **Chemist's: Farmácias** are open from 9 am to 1 pm and from 3 to 7 pm. Some are open all night and over the weekends and public holidays. The address of pharmacies on duty after normal shopping-hours can be found in daily newspapers and on the door of every other chemist's shop.

– **Health cover** – UK visitors should obtain the DHSS leaflet SA30 and certificate E111, which you must produce in case you need treatment in an emergency; this will be normally free at an official hospital. Medicines and dental treatment are not free. It is advisable to take out medical insurance, which you can do through your travel agent or insurance company.

– In order to say what part of your body is hurting, use the following expressions:
   Tenho uma dor no . . . (for masculine nouns)
   Tenho uma dor na . . . (for feminine words)

Parts of the body:

a	**cabeça** *head*	o	**braço** *arm*
os	**olhos** *eyes*	a	**mão** *hand*
o	**nariz** *nose*	o	**dedo** *finger*
os	**ouvidos** *ears*	o	**cotovelo** *elbow*
a	**boca** *mouth*	a	**perna** *leg*
o	**pescoço** *neck*	o	**pé** *foot*
a	**garganta** *throat*	o	**dedo do pé** *toe*
o	**dente** *tooth*	o	**joelho** *knee*

Answers

1 General Expressions
1 Sim. 2 Não. 3 Bom dia. 4 Como está a senhora?
5 Boa tarde. 6 Até à próxima. 7 Faz favor!
8 Obrigado (*if you are male*), Obrigada (*if you are female*)
9 De nada. 10 Com licença! 11 Desculpe. 12 Esta
mala de viagem é a minha. 13 É a minha mulher. 14 É o
meu marido. 15 Muito prazer. 16 O meu nome é . . . .

2 Arriving in Portugal
1 A mala de viagem (uma mala de viagem). 2 A mala de mão
(uma mala de mão). 3 Tem alguma coisa a declarar? 4 Não,
nada a declarar. 5 Abra a sua mala, faz favor. 6 Está bem.
Pode seguir. 7 O seu passaporte, f.f.. 8 A sua carta de
condução, f.f.. 9 O meu nome é . . ./Chamo-me . . . 10 Não,
estou aqui em férias. 11 Sim, sou inglês. 12 Não, sou
escocesa. 13 Grã-Bretanha. 14 Não compreendo.
15 Tem um jornal inglês?

3 Driving a Car
1 O carro (um carro). 2 o camião (um camião). 3 Super?
Normal? 4 Encha, f.f.. 5 Verifique o óleo e os pneus, f.f..
6 Boa viagem! 7 Auto-estrada. 8 Estrada Nacional 20.
9 Estacionamento/Parqueamento. 10 Estacionamento
proibido. 11 Bomba de gasolina. 12 Perigo.
13 Prioridade. 14 Pare.

4 Finding Your Way
1 Norte, Sul, Este/Leste, Oeste. 2 Uma planta de Lisboa, faz
favor. 3 Tem um mapa das estradas? 4 Onde fica a Praça
Marquês de Pombal, f.f.? 5 Qual é o caminho para Belém, f.f.?
6 Vire à direita. 7 Vire à esquerda. 8 Siga em frente.
9 É longe? 11 Siga à esquerda.

5 Public Transport
1 Informações. 2 Cacifos. 3 Bilheteira. 4 Um bilhete de
ida e volta para Coimbra, f.f.. 5 Vagão-restaurante.
6 Carruagem-cama. 7 Para o aeroporto, f.f.. 8 Partidas.
9 Onde é a paragem de autocarro? 10 Correspondência.
11 Saída. 12 Uma caderneta, f.f..

6 Accommodation
1 A cama (uma cama). 2 a chave (uma chave). 3 Há um
hotel bom aqui perto? 4 Tem um quarto vago? 5 Um

quarto com chuveiro para uma noite, f.f.. 6 Qual é o preço com pequeno almoço? 7 É muito caro. 8 Quero pagar. 9 O rés-do-chão. 10 Onde são os toiletes? 11 Livre. 12 Ocupado.

7 Numbers, Weights and Measures
1 Linha cinco. 2 Linha três. 3 Linha quatro. 4 Dez. 5 Quarenta e seis. 6 Cento e dezassete. 7 Duzentos e cinquenta e um. 8 Rua da República, oitenta e sete, mil e quinhentos Lisboa. 9 Cinco três, dois dois, zero um. 10 Duzentos e setenta e nove quilómetros. 11 Trezentos e dezoito km. 12 Duzentos e oitenta e dois km. 13 Trezentos e cinco km. 14 Duzentos e cinquenta gramas. 15 Um quilo. 16 Um litro de leite, f.f..

8 Times and Dates
1 Que horas são? 2 (a) São nove horas da manhã. (b) São seis horas e meia da manhã. (c) São sete horas e um quarto, da manhã. (d) São oito horas menos um quarto, da manhã. 3 (a) Vinte minutos; (b) Dez dias; (c) Duas semanas; (d) Dois meses. 4 Quando é que a senhora parte? 5 Amanhã à noite. 6 A que horas parte o avião? 7 De manhã, das oito horas e meia ao meio dia, de tarde, da uma hora às duas horas e meia. 8 Entre as catorze e as dezanove horas. 9 Trinta minutos. 10 Às vinte horas e quinze. 11 Às vinte e três horas e quinze. 12 Quinta-Feira, três de Dezembro.

9 Money and Shopping
1 Câmbio. 2 Que deseja? 3 Estou só a ver, obrigado/obrigada. 4 Tem T-shirts? 5 (a) Mil escudos. (b) Mil e quinhentos escudos. 6 Quanto é? 7 Mais alguma coisa? 8 Não, obrigado/obrigada. 9 Pague na caixa, f.f.. 10 Seis mil e dez escudos. 11 Oitenta e nove escudos e cinquenta centavos. 12 Seis mil e noventa e nove escudos e cinquenta centavos.

10 Meals
1 O pequeno almoço, o almoço e o jantar. 2 (a) o garfo; (b) o prato; (c) a faca; (d) a colher; (e) o copo; (f) a garrafa. 3 (a) o pãozinho; (b) a torrada. 4 Um chá com leite, f.f.. 5 Um sumo de fruta, f.f.. 6 Um copo de vinho, f.f.. 7 Uma sanduíche de queijo, f.f.. 8 Uma omeleta de fiambre, f.f..

nswers

Restaurants

(a) um restaurante; (b) um café ou um bar ou uma cervejaria;
) uma pastelaria/confeitaria. 2 (a) a cadeira (uma cadeira); (b)
mesa (uma mesa). 3 Tem uma mesa para dois (=para duas
·ssoas)? 4 A ementa e a carta dos vinhos, f.f.. 5 O prato do
a para um (=uma pessoa), f.f.. 6 Que deseja beber? 7 Faz
vor! Traga-me o azeite e o vinagre, f.f.. 8 (a) o queijo; (b) o
l; (c) a pimenta. 9 A conta, f.f.. 10 O troco é para si.

Starters, Meat, Fish

Uma costeleta, f.f.. 2 Um frango, f.f.. 3 Camarões, f.f..
Uma sopa de legumes, f.f.. 5 Uma sopa de tomate com ovo
calfado, f.f.. 6 Um bife bem passado, f.f.. 7 Um bife mal
assado, f.f.. 8 Pasta de fígado, f.f.. 9 Um ovo estrelado, f.f..
 Caldeirada para três, f.f..

Vegetables, Fruit, Desserts

Os feijões verdes. Gosto de feijões verdes. 2 A cebola. Gosto
: cebola. 3 As cenouras. Gosto de cenouras. 4 A maçã.
osto de maçãs. 5 Os figos. Gosto de figos. 6 A laranja.
osto de laranja. 7 As cerejas. Gosto de cerejas. 8 As uvas.
osto de uvas. 9 Os morangos. Gosto de morangos.
) Uma salada de tomate e alface, f.f.. 11 Morangos com
ata, f.f.. 12 Um sorvete(gelado) de baunilha e chocolate, f.f..

Drinking and Smoking

Um sumo de maçã, f.f.. 2 Uma laranjada, f.f.. 3 Duas
)las, f.f.. 4 Uma garrafa de água mineral, f.f.. 5 Dois
fés/Duas bicas, f.f.. 6 Um chá com leite e açúcar, f.f..
Um copo de vinho branco, f.f.. 8 Uma garrafa de vinho
nto, f.f.. 9 Uma imperial e um prato de tremoços, f.f.. 10 O
ca-rolhas. 11 A caixa de fósforos. 12 O maço de
garros. 13 O cinzeiro. 14 Deseja um cigarro?

Sightseeing and Entertainment

O Mosteiro dos Jerónimos. 2 A Torre de Belém.
O Padrão aos Descobrimentos. 4 Onde é o turismo, f.f.?
Desejo visitar o palácio. 6 Desejo ver a festa.
A que horas começa o espectáculo? 8 Horas de abertura.
Bilheteira. 10 Entrada. 11 Saída. 12 Fechado.

16 Excursions and Recreation

1 A Serra da Estrela. 2 Coimbra e o Rio Mondego.
3 Uma praia do Algarve. 4 Piscina. 5 Vestiário.
6 Desejo alugar um barco à vela. 7 O toldo. 8 A
barraca. 9 Uma máquina fotográfica, f.f.. 10 Um rolo, f.f..
11 Um flash, f.f..

17 The Weather

1 (a) Faz chuva e vento./Está a chover e faz vento. (b) Está
encoberto. (c) Faz sol. 2 (a) 28 graus; (b) 26 graus; (c) 29
graus. 3 Faz mau tempo. Faz chuva, vento e frio. 4 Faz
bom tempo. Faz sol e calor. 5 À 1.52 e às 14.17. 6 Às 7.45 e
às 19.57.

18 Post-Office and Telephone

1 Postais. 2 O marco do correio. 3 A carta. 4 O
selo. 5 O endereço. 6 A caneta. 7 Selos para dois postais
para Inglaterra, f.f.. 8 Qual é o número do seu telefone? 9 O
telefone. 10 Está lá? 11 É de . . .?

19 Clothing and Toiletries

1 Desejo . . . (a) uma blusa; (b) uma camisola; (c) uma camisa; (d)
uma saia; (e) um par de calças; (f) um par de sapatos; (g) um
chapéu; (h) um fato de banho; (i) um cinto. 2 Posso provar?
3 É pequeno. 4 Fico com este. 5 Tem uma escova para
dentes? 6 Tem uma pasta dentífrica? 7 Tem água de
colónia? 8 Tem uma máquina de barbear? 9 Tem óculos (de
sol)?

20 Accidents and Emergencies

1 Tenho o carro avariado. 2 Chame a polícia, f.f..
3 Houve um desastre. 4 A culpa não é minha. 5 Perdi o
passaporte. 6 Roubaram-me o porta-moedas. 7 Chame uma
ambulância, f.f.. 8 Tenho uma dor de dentes. 9 Tenho . . .
(a) uma dor de cabeça. (b) uma queimadura de sol. (c) febre.
10 Não é grave. 11 (a) Uma pomada, f.f.. (b) Pensos adesivos
f.f.. (c) Um medicamento/Um remédio, f.f.. 12 (a) Socorro! (b)
Pode ajudar-me!?

VOCABULARY

Portuguese-English Vocabulary

a the 1e
a, à(s), ao at 8b
aberto open 15d
abre-garrafas bottle opener 14b
acepipes appetizers 11b
acidente accident 20a
açúcar sugar 10c/11c
advogado lawyer 20c
aeroporto airport 5b
agência de viagens travel agency 15a
agora now 6c
Agosto August 8c
água water 3c/10b
água de colónia cologne 19d
aguaceiro shower 17c
ajudar help 20g
alcachofra artichokes 13a
aldeia village 4b
alface lettuce 13a
alfândega customs 2a
alguma coisa something 2a
alho garlic 13a
além beyond 8
alimentação grocer's 9
almoço lunch 10a
alugar hire 16c
aluguer de carros car hire 3a
amanhã tomorrow 8b
amarelo yellow 19c
ambulância ambulance 20f
amêijoas clams 12d
ameixa plum 13b
ananás pineapple 13b
andar floor 6b
ano year 8c
anticiclone high-pressure area 17b
apelido surname 2b
aperitivos appetizers 11b
apólice de seguro insurance papers 20a
aqui here 1f
armazém department store 9c
arroz rice 13a
as the 1e
ascensor lift 6b

ataque de coração heart attack 20d
até till 1b, as far as 7b
atenção caution 3b
atracções sights 15b
atraso delay 5e
auscultador receiver 18c
autocarro bus 5d
auto-estrada motorway 3b
autolocadora car rental 3a
auto-serviço self-service 9c
avaria breakdown 20a
avenida avenue 4c
avião aeroplane 5b
azeite olive oil 11c
azul blue 19c

bacalhau cod (dried) 12d
bagagem luggage 2a
banana banana 13b
banco 9b
bar bar 11a
barato cheap 9d
barbeiro barber 19e
barco boat, ship 5c
barco à vela sailing boat 16c
batatas potatoes 13a
batatas fritas chips/crisps 10d/13a
beber drink 10a
bebidas drinks 14a
bem well, o.k. 1a
bem passado well done 12b
bife (beef)steak 12b
bilhete ticket 5a/15d
bilhete de ida e volta return ticket 5a
bilheteira ticket office 5a ticket window 15d
boa noite good evening, good night, hello/goodbye 1b
boa tarde good afternoon, good evening, hello/goodbye 1b
boletim meteorológico weather report 17a
bolo cake 10d
bom good 1b

Portuguese-English Vocabulary

m dia good morning, hello/ goodbye 1b
mba de gasolina petrol filling station 3c
rrego lamb 12b
anco white 19c
itânico British 2c
onzeador suntan lotion 19d
onzear tan 16c
ate night club 15c

beleireiro hairdresser 19d
bina telefónica telephone box 18c
ça game 12b
cifos left luggage lockers 5a
deira chair 11a
fé coffee 10c, café, bar 11a
ixa cash desk 9d, box 14c
lção de banho swimming trunks 19a
lças trousers 19a
lor heat 17b
ma bed 6b
marões prawns 12d
marote cabin 5c
mbiar exchange 9b
mbio currency exchange 9b
mião lorry 3a
minho way, direction 4d
minhos de ferro railways 5a
mioneta coach 5d
misa shirt 19a
misola pullover, sweater 19a
neta pen 18b
ravana caravan 3a
rne meat 12b
ro expensive 6c
rro car 3a
rruagem-cama sleeping-car 5a
rta letter 18b
rta de condução driving licence 2b
rta dos vinhos wine list 11b
rtão de crédito credit card 9b
rteira wallet 20b
asa house 4b
asa de banho bathroom 6b

casaco jacket 19a
castanho brown 19c
castelo castle 15b
cavalheiros gents' 6d
cebola onion 13a
centro city/town centre 4b
cereja cherry 13b
cerveja beer 14b
chá tea 10c/14a
chama (como se chama?) what's your name? 2b
champanhe champagne 14b
chapéu hat 19a
chave key 1f/6b/20b
chávena cup 10b
chegada arrival 5e
cheio fully booked 6b
cheque de viagem traveller's cheque 9b
chocolate hot chocolate 10c
choque collision, crash 20a
chuva rain 17c
chuvada shower 17c
chuveiro shower 6b
cidade city, town 4b
cidra cider 14b
cinema cinema 15c
cinto belt 19a
cinzeiro ashtray 14c
cinzento grey 19c
coberta deck 5c
cobrar cash 9b
código postal postcode 18b
cogumelos mushrooms 13a
colans tights 19b
colher spoon 10b
com with 6c
comboio train 5a
começar begin 15c
comer eat 10a
como how 1b
comprar buy 9c
comprido long 19a
comprimido tablet 20e
confeitaria cake and snack shop 11a
constipação cold 20d
conservar keep 9

Portuguese-English Vocabulary

consulado consulate 2c
conta bill 6c
copo glass 10b
cor colour 19c
correio post office, post 18a
correspondência connections 5d
cortar cut 19e
costa coast 16b
costeleta chop 12b
couve cabbage 13a
cuidado caution 3b/20g
curto short 19a
curva bend 4d

declarar declare 2a
dentista dentist 20f
depósito de bagagem left
   luggage office 5a
depressa quickly 20f
depressão low-pressure area 17c
desastre accident 20a
desejo I wish, I'd like 9b,c/15b/
   16c/19b
desvio diversion 3b
devagar slowly 2c
dia day 8b
dinheiro money 9a
direita right 4d
doces sweets 13c
documentos do carro car
   registration papers 2b
doente ill 20d
domingo Sunday 8c
dor de cabeça headache 20d
duplo double 6b

e and 6b
elevador lift 6b
embaixada embassy 2c
ementa menu card 11b
empurrar, empurre push 15d
encoberto overcast 17c
endereço address 18b
entrada entrance 15d
entrada starter, hors d'hoeuvre
   11b
entre between 8
escada stairs 6b

Escócia Scotland 2c
escocês Scottish, Scotsman 2c
escocesa Scottish, Scotswoman
   2c
escova brush 19e
escova para dentes toothbrush
   19d
espectáculo performance 15c
esquerda left 4d
esqui aquático water skiing 16c
esta this, this one 1e
estação station 5a
estacionamento parking, car
   park 3d
estádio stadium 15c
este this, this one 1e
este east 4d
estrada road 3b
eu I 1f
excursão excursion, outing 16a
expedidor sender 18b

faca knife 10b
farmácia chemist's, pharmacy
   20e
fato de banho swimming
   costume 19a
favor, faz favor please, excuse
   me please 1c
fazer uma volta turística go on
   a sightseeing tour 4b
febre fever 20d
fechado closed 8c/15d
feijões verdes runner beans 13a
férias holiday 2b
ferido injured 20d
festa festival 15c
fiambre ham 10d
fica (é fica) is situated 4c
figo fig 13b
filme a cores colour film 16d
flash flash 16d
folheto brochure 15a
fósforo match 14c
foto, fotografia photo 16d
fralda nappy 19d
frango chicken 12c
frio cold 17d

Portuguese-English Vocabulary

fruta fruit 13b
fumar smoke 14c

galês Welsh, Welshman 2c
galesa Welsh, Welshwoman 2c
garagem garage 3d/20a
gare marítima embarkment area 5c
garfo fork 10b
garrafa bottle 10b/14b
gasóleo diesel 3c
gasolina petrol 3c
gelados ice cream, ice lollies 13c
geléia jam 10c
geléia de laranja marmalade 10c
gelo ice 17d
gorjeta tip 11d
gosto I like 13c/19a
grande big 19a
granizo hail 17c
grave serious 20f
grátis, gratuito free 9d
gruta cave 16b
guarda-chuva umbrella 17c
guardanapo napkin 10b
guia man/lady guide 15d

há there is, there are 6a
hoje today 8b
hoje à noite tonight 8b
hora hour, o'clock 8a
horário timetable 5e
horas de abertura opening hours 15d
hors d'oeuvre hors d'oeuvre, starter 11b
hospital hospital 20f
hotel hotel 6a

ida e volta return (ticket) 5a
igreja church 15b
impermeável raincoat 19a
impresso form 18b
indicativo area code 18c
informação information 5e
infracção offense 20c
inglês English, Englishman 2c

inglesa English, Englishwoman 2c
isqueiro lighter 14c

jantar dinner, supper 10a
jardim park, gardens 16b
jarro jug 10b
jornal newspaper 2c
Julho July 8c

ladrão thief 20b
lago lake 16b
laranja orange 13b
laranjada orangeade 14a
largo square 4c
legumes vegetables 12a/13a
leitaria dairy 9
leite milk 7b/14a
lenço scarf 19a, handkerchief 19d
lenços de papel paper tissues 19d
leste east 4d
libra pound sterling 9b
licor liqueur 14b
ligadura bandage 20e
limão lemon 10c/13b
limonada lemonade 14a
linguado sole 12d
linha track, platform 5a
lista menu card 11b
lista telefónica telephone book 18c
litoral coast 16b
livraria bookshop 9
livre free, for hire 5d, vacant 6d
loja shop 9c
loja de artesanato souvenir shop 9
loja de ferragens hardware shop 9
loja de lembranças souvenir shop 9
longe far 4d
lugar de hortaliça greengrocer's 9
luvas gloves 19a

Portuguese-English Vocabulary

maçã apple 13b
maço packet 14c
mal passado rare 12b
mala de mão handbag 2a
mala de viagem suitcase 1e
manhã morning 8a
manteiga butter 7b/10c
mapa map 4a
máquina de barbear electric razor 19d
máquina fotográfica camera 16d
mar sea 16b
marco do correio letter-box 18a
maré tide 17a
marido husband 1f
marisco shellfish 12d
mata wood 16b
mau bad 17c
medicamento medicine 20e
médico doctor 20f
médio medium 12b
meia garrafa half bottle 14b
meia-hora half an hour 8a
meia noite midnight 8b
meias socks, stockings 19b
meio dia noon 8b
melão melon 13b
menina girl 1d
menino boy 1d
mercado market 9c
mercearia grocer's, foodstore 9
mês month 8c
mesa table 11a
metro underground train 5d, metre 7b
meu (o meu) my, mine 1f
minha (a minha) my, mine 1f
miradouro vantage point 16a
moeda coin 9a
morangos strawberries 13b
motel motel 6a
muito very much 1c, a lot 7b
mulher wife 1f
mulheres women, ladies 6d
município town hall 4b
museu museum 15b

nadar swim 16c

nacionalidade nationality 2c
não no 1a/2a
nata cream 13c
negócios business 2b
neve snow 17d
nevoeiro fog 17c
no in the 4c
noite night, late evening 1b/6b/ 8b
nome name 1f/2b
norte north 4d
nublado cloudy 17c
número do telefone telephone number 18c
nuvem cloud 17c

o the 1e
obras road works 3b
obrigada, obrigado thank you 1c
óculos glasses 19d
ocupado engaged 6d
oeste west 4d
óleo oil 3c
onde where 4c/5d/6a/15a/18a
ontem yesterday 8b
os the 1e
ou or 14c
ovo egg 12c

padaria bakery 9
pagar pay 6c/9d
palácio palace 15b
pane breakdown 20a
pão bread 10c
pãozinho breadroll 10c
par de sapatos pair of shoes 19b
para to 5d, for 6b/11a/18b
paragem de autocarro bus-stop 5d
pare stop 3b
parque park 16b
parque de campismo camping site 6a
parqueamento parking, car park 3d
partida departure 5e

Portuguese-English Vocabulary

assaporte passport 1c/2b
asseio walk 16c
asta de fígado liver paté 12b
asta dentífrica toothpaste 19d
astelaria cake shop 11a
edir order 11b
eixaria fishmonger's 9
eixe fish 12d
ensão guesthouse 6a
enso adesivo sticking plaster 20e
enso higiénico sanitary towel 19d
ente comb 19e
equeno small 19a
equeno almoço breakfast 6c/10a
era pear 13b
erder lose 20b
erigo danger 3b/20g
erto near 4d
esca fishing 16c
eúgas socks 19b
ilha battery 16d
imenta pepper 11c
iscina swimming pool 16c
lanta streetmap 4a
neus tyres 3c
olícia police 20c, policeman 20c
omada ointment 20e
onte bridge 4d
orco pork 12b
orta-bagagem boot 2a
orta-moedas purse 20b
ortagem toll 3b
orto port 5c
ostal postcard 18b
osto de socorros first aid 20f
ouco (um pouco) a little 7b
ousada inn 6a
ousada de juventude youth hostel 6a
raça square 4c
raia beach 16c
rato plate, dish 10b/11b
reço price 6c/9d
reto black 19c

prioridade right of way 3b
puxar, puxe pull 15d

quando when 8b
quanto how much 3c/6c/9d
quantos how many 11a
quarto d'hora quarter of an hour 8a
quarta-feira Wednesday 8c
quarto room 6b
queijo cheese 10d/11b
queimadura de sol sunburn 20d
quente warm, hot 17b
quero I want, wish 6c
quinta-feira Thursday 8c
quiosque de jornais news-stand 9

recepção reception desk 6b
recibo receipt 9
reduzir marcha slow down 3b
refeição meal 10a
relógio watch, clock 8a
rés-do-chão ground floor 6b
reserva reservation 5a
residência place of residence 2b
rio river 16b
rocha rock 16b
rolo (de películas) film 16d
roubar steal 20b
roupa clothes 19a
rua street, urban road 4c

sábado Saturday 8c
sabonete toilet soap 19d
saca-rolhas corkscrew 14b
saco bag, carrier bag 2a
saia skirt 19a
saída exit 5d/20g
saída de emergência emergency exit 20g
sal salt 11c
sala de espera waiting room 5a
sala de jantar dining room 10a
salão de chá tea-shop 11a
salão de concertos concert hall 15c
sapateiro cobbler's 9

sapatos shoes 19b
segunda-feira Monday 8c
selo stamp 18b
sem without 10c
semáforo traffic lights 4c
semana week 8c
senor (o senhor) you 1b, gentleman 1d
senhora (a senhora) you 1b, lady 1d
senhoras ladies' 6d
senhores gents' 6d
sentido único one-way street 4c
serra mountain range 16b
serviço service 11d
seu (o seu) your, yours 1f
sexta-feira Friday 8c
shampô shampoo 19d
sim yes 1a
sobremesa dessert 11b
socorro! help! 20g
sol sun 17b
sombra shade 17b
sopa soup 12a
sorvete sorbet, ice cream 13c
sua (a sua) your, yours 1f
sul south 4d
sumo juice 10c/14a
supermercado supermarket 9c

tabacaria tobacconist 14c
taça dessert dish 10b
talho butcher's 9
tamanho size 19b
tarde afternoon, early evening 1b/8b
táxi taxi 5d

teatro theatre 15c
telefone telephone 18c
tempo weather 17a
terça-feira Tuesday 8c
tinto red (wine) 14b
toalha table cloth 10b, towel 19d
todos os dias every day 8b
toiletes toilets 6d
torre tower 15b
trabalhos róad works 3b
trânsito traffic 3a
troco small change 9a
trovoada thunderstorm 17c
turismo tourist information 15a

um a, an 1e
uma a, an 1e
uvas grapes 13b

vaca beef 12b
vagão-restaurante dining car 5a
vago vacant, free 6b/11a
veículos pesados heavy vehicles 3a
vento wind 17c
verde green 19c
vermelho red 19c
vestido dress, frock 19a
vinho wine 14b
visitar visit 15b
vitela veal 12b
volta tour 16a
vôo flight 5b

zona de peões pedestrian zone 4c

English-Portuguese Vocabulary

a um 1e
accident acidente, desastre 20a
address endereço 18b
aeroplane avião 5b
afternoon tarde 8b
airport aeroporto 5b
a little um pouco 7b
a lot muito 7b
ambulance ambulância 20f
an um 1e
and e 6b
anything alguma coisa 2a
appetizer aperitivos, acepipes 11b
apple maçã 13b
area code indicativo 18c
arrival chegada 5e
artichoke alcachofra 13a
ashtray cinzeiro 14c
at a, à(s), ao 8b
August Agosto 8c
avenue avenida 4c

bad mau 17c
bag saco 2a
bakery padaria 9
banana banana 13b
bandage ligadura 20f
bank banco 9b
bar bar 11a
barber barbeiro 19e
bathroom casa de banho 6b
battery pilha 16d
beach praia 16c
bed cama 6b
beef vaca 12b
beefsteak bife 12b
beer cerveja 14b
begin começar 15c
belt cinto 19a
bend curva 4d
big grande 19a
bill conta 6c
black preto 19c
blue azul 19c
boat barco 5c
bookshop livraria 9
boot porta-bagagem 2a

bottle garrafa 10b/14b
bottle opener abre-garrafas 14b
boulevard avenida 4c
box caixa 14c
boy menino 1d
bread pão 10c
bread roll pãozinho 10c
breakdown pane, avaria 10a
breakfast pequeno almoço 6c/10a
bridge ponte 4c
British britânico 2c
brochure folheto 15a
brown castanho 19c
brush escova 19e
bus autocarro 5d
bus stop paragem de autocarro 5d
business negócios 2b
butcher's talho 9
butter manteiga 7c/10c
buy comprar 9c

cabbage couve 13a
cabin camarote 5c
café café 11a
cake bolo 10d
cake shop pastelaria, confeitaria 11a
camera máquina fotográfica 16d
camp site parque de campismo 6a
car carro 3a
caravan caravana 3a
car registration papers documentos do carro 2b
car rental aluguer de carros 3a
cash cobrar 9b
cashdesk caixa 9d
castle castelo 15b
caution atenção 3b/20g
cave gruta 16b
chair cadeira 11a
champagne champanhe 14b
change cambiar 9b
cheap barato 9d

English-Portuguese Vocabulary

cheese queijo 10d/11b
chemist's farmácia 20f
cherry cereja 13b
chicken frango 12c
chips batatas fritas 10a/13a
chocolate chocolate 10c
chop costeleta 12b
church igreja 15b
cider cidra 14b
cinema cinema 15c
city cidade 4b
city centre centro 4b
clams amêijoas 12d
clock relógio 8a
closed fechado 8c/15d
clothes roupa 19a
cloud nuvem 17c
cloudy nublado 17c
coach camioneta 5d
coast costa, litoral 16b
coat casaco 19a
cobbler's sapateiro 9
cod bacalhau 12c
coffee café 10c/14a
coin moeda 9a
cold frio 17d, constipação 20e
collision choque 20a
Cologne água de colónia 19d
colour cor 19c
comb pente 19e
concert hall sala de concertos 15c
connections correspondência 5d
consulate consulado 2c
corkscrew saca-rolhas 14b
cream nata 13c
credit card cartão de crédito 9b
cup chávena 10b
currency exchange câmbio 9b
customs alfândega 2a
cut cortar 19e

dairy leitaria 9
danger perigo 3b/20g
day dia 8b
deck coberta 5c
declare declarar 2a
delay atraso 5e

dentist dentista 20f
department store armazém 9c
departure partida 5e
dessert sobremesa 11b
dessert dish taça 10b
diesel gasóleo 3c
dining car vagão-restaurante 5a
dining room sala de jantar 10a
dinner jantar 10a
direction caminho 4d
dish prato 10b/11b
diversion desvio 3b
doctor médico 20f
dress vestido 19a
drink beber 10a
drinks bebidas 14a
driving licence carteira de condução 2b
double duplo 6b

east este, leste 4d
eat comer 10a
egg ovo 12c
electric razor máquina de barbear 19d
embarkment area gare 5c
embassy embaixada 2c
emergency exit saída de emergência 20g
engaged ocupado 6d
England Inglaterra 2c
English inglês, inglesa 2c
English(man) inglês 2c
English(woman) inglesa 2c
entrance entrada 15d
evening tarde, noite 8b
every day todos os dias 8b
excursion excursão 16a
exit saída 5d/20g
expensive caro 6c
express train expresso 5a

far longe 4d
far, as far as até 7b
festival festa 4d
fever febre 20d
fig figo 13b

English-Portuguese Vocabulary

ilm filme, rolo (de películas) 16d
inger dedo 20
irst aid posto de socorros 20f
ish peixe 12d
ishing pesca 16c
ishmonger's peixaria 9
lash flash 16d
light vôo 5b
loor andar 6b
og nevoeiro 17c
oodstore alimentação 9
or para 6b/11a/18b
ork garfo 10b
orm impresso 18b
ree livre 5d, vago 6b/11a, gratuito 9d
Friday sexta-feira 8c
ruit fruta 13b
ully booked cheio 6b

game caça 12b
garage garagem 3d/20a
garlic alho 13a
gents' senhores, homens, cavalheiros 6d
girl menina 1d
glass copo 10b
glasses óculos 19d
glove luva 19a
good bom 1b/17b
good afternoon boa tarde 1b
goodbye bom dia, boa tarde, boa noite 1b
good morning bom dia 1b
grapes uvas 13b
grey cinzento 19c
green verde 19c
greengrocer's lugar de hortaliça 9
grocer's mercearia, alimentação 9
ground floor rés-do-chão 6b
guest house pensão 6a
guide guia 15d

hail granizo 17c
haircut cortar 19e

hairdresser cabeleireiro 19e
half an hour meia-hora 8a
half-bottle meia garrafa 14b
ham fiambre 10d
hand mão 20
handbag mala de mão 2a
handkerchief lenço 19d
hardware shop loja de ferragens 9
hat chapéu 19a
headache dor de cabeça 20d
heart attack ataque de coração 20d
heavy vehicles veículos pesados 3a
hello bom dia, boa tarde, boa noite 1b; está lá? 18c
help ajudar, socorro 20g
here aqui 1f
high-pressure area anticiclone 17b
hire alugar 16c
holiday férias 2b
hospital hospital 20f
hot quente 17b
hotel hotel 6a
hour hora 8a
house casa 4b
how como 1b
how many quantos 7b/11a
how much quanto 3c/6c/9d
hurt ferido 20d
husband marido 1f

I eu 1f
ice gelo 17d
ice cream sorvete, gelado 13d
ice lolly gelado 13d
ill doente 20d
information informação 5e
injured ferido 20d
inn pousada, estalagem 6a
insurance apólice de seguro 20a

jacket casaco 19a
jam geléia 10c
jug jarro 10b
juice sumo 10c/14a

English-Portuguese Vocabulary

July Julho 8c

key chave 1f/6b/20b
knife faca 10b

ladies' senhoras, mulheres 6d
lake lago 16b
lamb borrego 12b
lawyer advogado 20c
left esquerda 4d
left luggage depósito de
  bagagem 5a
lemon limão 10c/13b
lemonade limonada 14a
letter carta 18b
letter box marco do correio 18a
lettuce alface 13a
lift ascensor, elevador 6b
lighter isqueiro 14c
like (I like = I enjoy, I'm keen
  on) gosto 13c/19a
like (I'd like) desejo 9b,c/15b/
  16c/19b
liqueur licor 14b
liver paté pasta de fígado 12b
lockers cacifos 5a
long comprido 19a
lorry camião 3a
lose perder 20b
low-pressure area depressão 17c
luggage bagagem 2a
lunch almoço 10a

map mapa 4a
market mercado 9c
marmalade geléia de
  laranja 10c
match fósforo 14c
meal refeição 10a
meat carne 12b
medicine medicamento,
  remédio 20e
medium médio 12b
melon melão 13b
men homens 6d
menu ementa, lista 11b
midnight meia-noite 8b
milk leite 7b/10c/14a

Monday segunda-feira 8c
money dinheiro 9a
month mês 8c
morning manhã 8a
motorway auto-estrada 3b
motel motel 6a
mountain range serra 16b
Mr Sr. (Senhor) 1d
Mrs Sr.ª D. (Senhora Dona) 1d
museum museu 15b
mushroom cogumelo 13a
my o meu, a minha 1f

name nome 1f/2b
napkin guardanapo 10b
nappy fralda 19d
nationality nacionalidade 2c
near perto 4d
newspaper jornal 2c
news-stand quiosque de jornais
  9
night noite 6b/8b
night club buate 15c
no não 1a/2a
noon meio-dia 8b
north norte 4d
now agora 6c

offence infracção 20c
oil óleo 3c
ointment pomada 20e
olive oil azeite 11c
one-way street sentido único 4c
onion cebola 13a
open aberto 15d
opening hours horas de
  abertura 15d
or ou 14c
orange laranja 13b
orangeade laranjada 14a
order pedir 11b
outing excursão 16a
overcast encoberto 17c

packet of cigarettes maço de
  cigarros 14c
pair of shoes par de
  sapatos 19b

English-Portuguese Vocabulary

palace palácio 15b
park jardim, parque 16b
parking estacionamento,
  parqueamento 3d
passport passaporte 2b
pay pagar 6c/9d
pear pera 13b
pen caneta 18b
pepper pimenta 11c
performance espectáculo 15c
petrol gasolina 3c
petrol filling station bomba de
  gasolina 3c
pharmacy farmácia 20f
photo fotografia, foto 16d
pineapple ananás 13b
place of residence residência 2b
plaster penso adesivo 20e
plate prato 10b
platform linha 5a
please faz favor 1c
plum ameixa 13b
police polícia 20c
policeman polícia 20c
pork porco 12b
port porto 5c
Portuguese português,
  portuguesa 2c
Portuguese man português 2c
Portuguese woman portuguesa
  2c
postcard postal 18b
post code código postal 18b
post office correio 18a
potatoes batatas 13a
pound libra 9b
prawns camarões 12d
price preço 6c/9d
pull puxar, puxe 15d
purse porta-moedas 20b
push empurrar, empurre 15d

quarter of an hour quarto
  d'hora 8a
quickly depressa 20f

raincoat impermeável 19a
railways caminhos de ferro 5a

rain chuva 17c
rare mal passado 12b
receiver auscultador 18c
reception desk recepção 6b
red vermelho 19c, tinto 14b
reservation reserva 5a
return (ticket) ida e volta 5a
rice arroz 13a
right direita 4d
right-of-way prioridade 3b
river rio 16b
road estrada 3b
road toll portagem 3b
road works obras, trabalhos 3b
rock rocha 16b
room quarto 6b
runner beans feijões verdes 13a

sailing boat barco à vela 16c
salt sal 11c
sanitary towel penso higiénico
  19d
Saturday sábado 8c
scarf lenço 19a
Scotland Escócia 2c
Scottish escocês, escocesa 2c
Scotsman escocês 2c
Scotswoman escocesa 2c
sea mar 16b
see ver 15b
self-service auto-serviço 9c
sender expedidor 18b
serious grave 20f
service serviço 11d
service station bomba de
  gasolina 3c
shade sombra 17b
shampoo shampô 19d
shellfish marisco 12d
ship barco 5c
shirt camisola 9a, camisa 19a
shoes sapatos 19b
shop loja 9c
short curto 19a
shower chuveiro 6b, chuvada,
  aguaceiro 17c
sights atracções 15b

English-Portuguese Vocabulary

sightseeing tour volta turística 4b
size tamanho 19b
skirt saia 19a
sleeping car carruagem-cama 5a
slow down reduzir marcha 3b
slowly devagar 2c
small pequeno 19a
small change troco 9a
smoke fumar 14c
snow neve 17d
socks peúgas, meias 19b
sole linguado 12d
soup sopa 12a
south sul 4d
souvenir shop loja de lembranças, loja de artesanato 9
spoon colher 10b
square largo, praça 4c
stadium estádio 15c
stairs escada 6b
stamp selo 18b
station estação 5a
steak bife 12b
steal roubar 20b
stockings meias 19b
storey andar 6b
stop pare 3b
straight ahead em frente 4d
strawberry morango 13b
street rua 4c
street map planta 4a
stroll passeio 16c
sugar açúcar 10c/11c
suitcase mala de viagem 1e
sun sol 17b
sunburn queimadura de sol 20d
Sunday domingo 8c
suntan lotion bronzeador 19d
supermarket supermercado 9c
supper jantar 10a
surname apelido 2b
sweater camisola 19a
sweet doce 13c
swim nadar 16c

swimming trunks calção de banho 19a
swimming costume fato de banho 19a
swimming pool piscina 16c

table mesa 11a
tablecloth toalha 10b
tablet comprimido 20e
tan bronzear 16c
taxi táxi 5d
tea chá 10c/14a
tea shop salão de chá 11a
teeth dentes 20d
telephone book lista telefónica 18c
telephone box cabina telefónica 18c
telephone number número de telefone 18c
thank you obrigado, obrigada 1c/9c
the o, a, os, as 1e
theatre teatro 15c
thief ladrão 20b
this este, esta 1e
thunderstorm trovoada 17c
Thursday quinta-feira 8c
ticket bilhete 5a/15d
ticket office bilheteira 5a
ticket window bilheteira 15d
tide maré 17a
tights colans 19b
till até 1b
timetable horário 5e
tip gorjeta 11d
tissues lenços de papel 19d
to para 5d
tobacconist tabacaria 14c
today hoje 8b
toilets toiletes, WC 6d, casa de banho 6
tomorrow amanhã 8b
tonight hoje à noite 8b
toothbrush escova para dentes 19d
toothpaste pasta dentífrica 19d
tour visitar 15d, volta 16a

English-Portuguese Vocabulary

tourist information office turismo 15a
towel toalha 19d
tower torre 15b
town cidade 4b
town hall município 4b
track linha 5a
traffic trânsito 3a
traffic lights semáforo 4c
train comboio 5a
travel agency agência de viagens 15a
traveller's cheque cheque de viagem 9b
trip viagem 1e
trousers calças 19a
truck camião 3a
Tuesday terça-feira 8c
tyres pneus 3c
toilet soap sabonete 19d

umbrella guarda-chuva 17c
underground metro 5d
underground station estação do metro 5d

vacant livre 6d
vantage point miradouro 16a
veal vitela 12b
vegetables legumes 13a
very much muito 1c
village aldeia 4b
visit visitar 15d

waiting room sala de espera 5a
Wales País de Gales 2c
walk passeio 16c
wallet carteira 20b
want (I want) quero 6c

want (I want = I need) preciso 20a
warm quente 17b
watch relógio 8a
water água 3b/10b
water skiing esqui aquático 16c
way caminho 4d
weather tempo 17a
weather report boletim meteorológico 17a
Wednesday quarta-feira 8c
week semana 8c
well bem 1a/2a
well-done bem passado 12b
Welsh galês, galesa 2c
west oeste 4d
when quando 8b
where onde 4c/5d/6a/15a/18a
white branco 19c
wife mulher 1f
wind vento 17c
wine vinho 10b/14b
wine list carta dos vinhos 11b
wish (I wish) desejo, quero 9b,c/ 15b/16c/19b
with com 6b
without sem 10c
woman mulher 1d
wood mata 16b

year ano 8c
yellow amarelo 19c
yes sim 1a
yesterday ontem 8b
you o senhor, a senhora 1f
your o seu, a sua 1f
youth hostel pousada de juventude 6a

First published 1988
Copyright © 1988 Manuela Cook and Langenscheidt KG

Illustrations by Herbert Horn.

British Library Cataloguing in Publication Data
Cook, Manuela
    Quick & easy Portuguese.—(Teach yourself
    books).
    1. Spoken Portuguese language
    I. Title
    469.83′421

ISBN 0 340 48963 4

Printed and bound in Great Britain for
Hodder and Stoughton Educational,
a division of Hodder and Stoughton Ltd,
Mill Road, Dunton Green, Sevenoaks, Kent,
by Richard Clay Ltd, Bungay, Suffolk

Phototypeset by Cotswold Typesetting Ltd, Gloucester